Lively Sacrifice

Also by Michael Perham and published by SPCK:

Liturgy Pastoral and Parochial (1984)
Waiting for the Risen Christ
(with Kenneth Stevenson, 1986)
Towards Liturgy 2000 (editor, 1989)
Welcoming the Light of Christ
(with Kenneth Stevenson, 1991)
Liturgy for a New Century (editor, 1991)
Enriching the Christian Year (1993)
Model and Inspiration (editor, 1993)
The Renewal of Common Prayer (editor, 1993)

LIVELY SACRIFICE

The Eucharist in the
Church of England today

Michael Perham

First published in Great Britain 1992
SPCK
Holy Trinity Church
Marylebone Road
London NW1 4DU

Second impression 1994

© Michael Perham 1992

British Library Cataloguing-in-Publication Data

CIP data for this book is available from the British Library

ISBN 0-281-04618-2

Typeset by Pioneer Associates Ltd, Perthshire
Printed and bound in Great Britain by
Biddles Ltd, Guildford and King's Lynn

*For my Father and my Mother
from whom I first learned
to value the Eucharist*

CONTENTS

CONTENTS

PART IV

PREFACE

In 1978, encouraged by the late Geoffrey Cuming, who had been my liturgy tutor at Cuddesdon, I wrote a little book entitled *The Eucharist*, which was published by SPCK and the Alcuin Club. When, four years later, I wrote *Liturgy Pastoral and Parochial* (SPCK 1984), which has a much broader sweep, I did not devote many pages to the celebration of the Eucharist, referring the reader back to the earlier book. *Liturgy Pastoral and Parochial* is still available and still being bought, but people cannot refer back to *The Eucharist*, which is now both unavailable and dated in its approach. It was written before the appearance of the Alternative Service Book, and even its second edition in 1981 could not draw on years of experience of using that book. I do not stand today by everything I wrote then.

Lively Sacrifice is in one way the successor to *The Eucharist*, though I have drawn on the material there only slightly, and this is in most ways a different sort of book. I hope it has a good deal of objectivity, and that its theology and its liturgy are sound. It is nevertheless a very personal statement, giving me the opportunity to express convictions about the Eucharist that are passionately held.

I have wanted to write this book because the Eucharist is central to my life as a Christian and a priest. I never tire of its celebration, whether I am at the altar or in the pew. It is the source of much joy and gladness. Yet so often I sense that it falls far short of what it could be for Christian people, in terms of deepening their relationship with God, feeding them spiritually, and equipping them for daily life. How the Eucharist is understood and how

it is celebrated has implications for their souls. Whether
they be daily communicants, or weekly, or monthly, if
they are serious about what they are doing, and if what
they encounter every time they come to worship helps
them to grow, then the Eucharist becomes a powerful
tool in the formation of their spirituality and gives shape
to their lifestyle. But when what they encounter is life-
denying or slipshod, not only have opportunities been
lost, but harm has been done.

Sometimes it seems that we approach the preparation
and celebration of the Eucharist unaware that it can
change lives and shape them too. I would like to think
that this book might make a small contribution in raising
the level of that awareness.

But, as well as communicating something of my
enthusiasm and thankfulness for the Eucharist, I have
wanted also to contribute creatively to some of the
tensions in the celebration of the liturgy in the Church of
England today, not least because I feel some of those
tensions and contradictions within myself.

There is what sometimes seems a great divide between
'Prayer Book people', deeply loyal to the Book of
Common Prayer of 1662, and those who espouse new
liturgies, sometimes with an impatience for the old order.
I find myself sympathetic to both, and wanting to help
them to listen to one another.

There are the different emphases that arise from
backgrounds of churchmanship. I have a love for the
symbol and ritual of the Catholic tradition, and my own
spirituality, poor as it may be, has been much sustained
by it. I have also come to value the insights brought to
the Church by Evangelicals and by those deeply
influenced by the Renewal Movement, and I am
profoundly glad that the worship of so many Christians
like myself, who do not think of themselves as
'charismatic' in the more precise sense, has nevertheless
been wonderfully opened up and liberated through the
Spirit's work in them. But I also retain an instinctive feel
for the distinct character and ethos of Anglican liturgy,

and I do not believe that the Church of England will be well served if that is jettisoned today.

There is also the related tension between, on the one hand, the desire for liturgical variety and freedom and, on the other, the quest for contemporary common prayer, with the limitation to diversity that that must impose.

All these tensions are not simply ones that I observe, but ones that I feel inside me and experience in my ministry, and so, in wrestling with them in a book, I have to reveal a little of my own contradictions and hopes.

Some of what is written here has come out before in talks and lectures. In particular I am grateful to Patrick Harris, the Bishop of Southwell, for inviting me to share with the clergy and lay people of his diocese in the autumn of 1991 some thoughts about worship and evangelism, much of which has found a place in this book. Inevitably there is also some overlap with some of the material in *Liturgy Pastoral and Parochial*, though I have hardly opened it in writing afresh. There is also a lot of the thinking of my colleagues in the Liturgical Commission here too, not that I have consciously stolen other people's ideas and insights, though I have learned a good deal from listening to wise and scholarly men and women among my friends, and, if there is anything good here, some of it will have come from them.

But one learns about worship more by sharing in it than by discussing it, and it has been my privilege through the last eight years to worship with the people of the three churches of the parish where I have been team rector – St George's Church, Oakdale, St Paul's Church, Canford Heath, and Christ Church, Creekmoor. To all the people in those churches, and particularly to those specially involved in the liturgy (my fellow priests and deacons and lay ministers of different kinds), I owe a deep debt of gratitude. In their company it has always been a joy, as well as a duty, to worship at the Eucharist.

I also express grateful thanks to Judith Longman,

Editorial Director at SPCK, who has been enthusiastic about this book from when it was first proposed, to Jane Sinclair and David Stancliffe, who both found time to read my manuscript and made helpful suggestions, to my parents, in whose home in Dorchester I was given the peace and quiet to write this book during January 1992, and to my wife, Alison, who has encouraged me and helped create the space for the work to be done, believing as much as I do that, whenever Christian people gather for the Eucharist, it needs to be in every way a 'lively sacrifice'.

Michael Perham

Oakdale, Poole

Candlemas 1992

PART I

1

GRASPING THE HEEL OF HEAVEN

Lively Sacrifice

> And here we offer and present unto thee, O Lord, ourselves, our souls and bodies, to be a reasonable, holy, and lively sacrifice unto thee.

One of the great delights of the Prayer Book Communion rite has always been the 'lively sacrifice' of which it speaks, as indeed it does also of God's 'true and lively word' earlier in the service. Ever since the Proposed Prayer Book of 1928, life has not been the same, for that book made a change, in the interests of plain meaning, and *'lively* sacrifice' became *'living* sacrifice'. For all its intelligibility, and its faithfulness to St Paul's meaning in Romans 12, it loses something. It is much the same with 'liveth and reigneth', which modern Roman liturgy translates as 'lives and reigns', and misses the point. It is not that Christ lives (as if the phrase were about his domicile) but that he is alive, the risen Lord. So also the Eucharist is a sacrifice about being alive. It is the celebration of the Lord in our midst who is very much alive. It is also about the offering of our souls and bodies, of everything that makes us alive to God, to his world and to each other. And, if it is that, I believe it will also be, in the ordinary everyday sense of the word, *lively*. When we encounter the Eucharist, and it isn't teeming with life, something has gone wrong.

Yet the Prayer Book phrase is 'lively sacrifice', and the word 'sacrifice' needs to stay there too as a corrective. Many are the books that have been written about the word 'sacrifice' in relation to the Eucharist. This is not another of them. I hold to that essentially Anglican

position that is a little uncomfortable with some of the
Roman Catholic language of sacrifice in the Mass, and
not unsympathetic to the Reformers' concern that
nothing should detract from the unique once-for-all
sacrifice of Calvary, but which is happy to use the word
sacrifice of the Eucharist, and to see in it self-offering
linking the communicant with the offering of Christ.

But my concern to retain the word here, as a
corrective, is lest our modern eucharistic worship should
lose the sharp cutting edge of the cross. That danger
does seem real in the style of some celebrations.

The danger is there in the very word 'celebration'. It is
not new to the Christian vocabulary. Anglicans of an
earlier generation sometimes spoke of 'going to the early
celebration', and they were certainly not expecting
anything very lively. They spoke of the priest at the
Eucharist as 'the celebrant', though now we are rightly
bidden to remember that in the celebration of the
Eucharist it is the whole people of God who are the
celebrants, and the priest is merely the one among them
who presides. If we use the word 'celebration' more
today to describe worship (and not just the Eucharist),
it is because we have been recovering a sense of freedom,
joy and life that somehow seemed to have been lost.
Sometimes this liveliness has a superficiality to it, a
kind of surface bubble without much depth, but it need
not be so, and many churches where the worship is very
much alive are churches where there is a very serious
sense of waiting upon the Holy Spirit, and the liveliness
comes from being open to that influence which renews
and deepens.

Yet I am still grateful that it is a lively *sacrifice*, for if
anything is to prevent the decline into a banal kind of
jollity, which is no substitute for deep Christian joy, it is
the cross. It is the cross, the sacrifice, that lies at the
heart of the eucharistic celebration. It is the cross that
means that every time we come to worship there will
needs be an element of penitence in our approach. It is
the cross that means that those who come to church,

burdened with sadnesses and sicknesses of many kinds, for whom celebration is not the immediate mood at all, can come to Christ and find his yoke is easy and his burden light.

Those with least time for the Reformation Communion rites, including the Church of England's Prayer Book rite of 1662, often point to the imbalance whereby the cross so dominates, that other elements of the Christian story – creation, incarnation, resurrection – are almost squeezed out. That is indeed an imbalance, and we can be grateful that it has been remedied. Yet we need to be wary, lest in redressing the imbalance, we lose sight of how the cross must have central place if we are to be true to our tradition and if the Eucharist is to be both a comfortable word and a challenging word. It isn't just a party.

Freedom and order

One of the areas in which there is controversy in the Church today is that of freedom and order in worship. There is an unnecessary tendency to draw a contrast between openness to the Spirit of God and concern with good order. The matter can be presented in such a way that those who are concerned with order are branded as those who follow the letter of the law, which kills real worship, while those who are free of that follow the Spirit who gives life. Undoubtedly there is a legalistic mind that can creep into the ordering of worship, and the Church of England, with its elaborate parliamentary and synodical procedures for authorizing forms of service, is prone to it. But, on the whole, a concern for good order is in reality a concern to create the conditions in which people feel free and open to receive what God is always offering.

The basis of much liturgical thinking today is the need to provide sufficient shape and structure to worship that people are secure enough to benefit from the spontaneous and the unfamiliar (which is very often the moment

when the Spirit of God seems most at work). Where
people are lost, perplexed or even (if their traditional
landmarks have been removed) angry, there is not likely
to be an openness to the Spirit of God. There are
occasions, of course, when it is right that liturgy should
shake and disturb, but that is not the way that it
normally draws people to God. They deepen their
spirituality from the sound basis of a shape and a
structure, and even a set of texts, that are familiar,
reassuring and well-tried. With that sort of security,
they can be open, imaginative and bold. Order is, for
most people most of the time, the pre-condition for
spontaneity and freedom. The liturgist, with his or her
concern for satisfying structures, is in league with the
Spirit.

There are many who would recognize some truth in
that when it comes to broad principles about shape and
structure, but some would be doubtful about a concern
with liturgical order that ended up in prescribing details.
'Should the president stand or sit during the Prayers of
Intercession?' 'Should the *Gloria* be said on the feast
day of a martyr in Lent?' 'May a lay person read the
gospel at the Eucharist?' Do these questions matter? At
one level, of course, the answer has to be No. No
fundamental Christian principle is at stake. No one's
eternal salvation is under threat for not knowing the
answer. Yet there is a sense in which, if some of this
detail contributes to the creation of a liturgy that is
deeply satisfying, these matters are not to be despised.

Ordinary churchgoers are not aware of the rules by
which the liturgist works. They ought not be aware of
them. If they were, these rules would be an intrusion
into worship. In some ways that is why clergy and
others who do know these rules find it so much more
difficult to worship – there are so many more things
that can irritate them if they are not to their taste. But
ordinary churchgoers can often know by instinct that a
service doesn't feel quite right, hasn't come together in a
way that creates deep prayerfulness or a sense of the

presence of God. And the reason that has not happened is sometimes that those planning it ignored the rules of good liturgical practice. There was the intrusion of a text introducing a change of mood when it wasn't time for it. There was an imbalance in the way the parts of the service were shared between leaders. There were no climaxes or there were too many. Application of some rule-of-thumb liturgical principles might have ironed those out and created the kind of worship where everything humanly possible came together to open up the people to the Spirit of God yearning to come in. I believe the detail can make its humble contribution to the noble enterprise of helping Christian people to be in touch with their Creator.

When people go to the theatre or the ballet, they do not want to be aware of the stage directions. But they know it would be a chaotic and unsatisfactory experience if there were none. It is strange that we can sometimes be suspicious about the use of words like 'drama' and 'theatre' in relation to the worship of the Church. Of course liturgy cannot only be drama or theatre, of course it must never be only performance, but it cannot be *less* than any of those things. The liturgy is the drama that celebrates the story of our salvation, nothing less, and the attention to detail must be such that we are all caught up in it, never audience, always participants.

Therefore with angels

Some of this presupposes that we know the purpose of worship. What is it for? What are we trying to do? The word 'trying' has its problems, for at a very fundamental level we are not 'trying' to do anything at all. We worship because that is a deep human instinct within us. We worship because the Spirit of God conspires with our human spirit to bring us into a relationship with the Father through Christ. The story of Christian history confirms that the instinct to worship God has never been capable of suppression for long. We are not trying, we are doing what we have to do, we are doing what comes naturally for us. Yet, for all its inadequacy, it is important to press the question: What is it we are trying to do?

To look at different Christian communities as they prepare and celebrate their Sunday worship is to get some strange answers. There are some churches where it looks very much as if the major aim of the Sunday service is to evangelize. The service has been put together with a conscious intention of drawing into faith, maybe by a powerful challenge, those not already committed. I do not doubt for a moment that worship is a highly effective means of evangelism. But I doubt very much if it is what we should set out to do each Sunday morning.

Or there are churches where it looks as if the major aim of worship is to teach. Anglicans in the past have been very ready for such an approach, for they have come to 'hear the sermon' more than anything else. Nowadays it may be dividing into buzz groups or looking at diagrams on the overhead projector, but the intention is the same – to teach. Again this is very important, and I do not doubt that the liturgy is itself a great teacher, but is teaching what we are trying to do?

In a third sort of church the emphasis seems to be on the building up of a sense of community. Here again, there is no doubt that true worship does engender a deep sense of fellowship, but it is not what we set out to achieve. This third sort of church illustrates how the pursuit of a lesser objective may blind that church to what is most needed. What really creates fellowship in a church community is faith deeply held and shared. While the vicar is busy exhorting people to be friendly, to share the Peace more enthusiastically, and to be sure to come to coffee after the service, he may be missing the point that what is needed in that church is a deep experience of the living God. If they had that, they would have something to talk about after the service, and might even flock to coffee to do so!

The truth is that the deep purpose of worship is not to

evangelize, nor to teach, nor to engender fellowship, but to be in touch with the living God. I believe that worship is for worship, and not primarily for anything else. Worship is to enable us to reach up to grasp the heel of heaven, to glimpse, albeit imperfectly and fleetingly, the life of heaven, to plug in, for a moment, to the worship of the angels and the praises of the saints. However and wherever the 'Holy, holy, holy . . .' found its way into the Eucharist, it deserves to stay there for all time, if for no other reason than to remind us, every time we come, that we do not create worship; we simply join ourselves for a while to the perpetual worship around the throne of God.

> Therefore with angels and archangels,
> and with all the company of heaven,
> we proclaim your great and glorious name,
> for ever praising you and saying:
> Holy, holy, holy Lord,
> God of power and might,
> heaven and earth are full of your glory.
> Hosanna in the highest.

My worry is not that our worship so often falls short of this. Our sinful human nature makes it inevitable that we shall, most of the time, remain fairly earthbound, and indeed there is a sense in which our feet ought to be firmly grounded on this earth, even though our hearts are to be up in heaven. No, I am not worried that we fail to find ourselves caught up in the holiness around the throne of God at every Eucharist. My worry is that we are not expecting it to happen ever. We are not yearning for it. We have lost sight of it as the crown of our worshipping endeavour. I believe that our worship will be of little avail, and certainly will have little chance of being lively sacrifice, until we have rebuilt that expectation in priest and people alike. Of course it will not happen to everybody every day. Of course it will rarely be a vision of God in all his beauty, and nearly always grasping the heel is the nearest we shall get. But

we must not settle for less than a yearning to be touched
by the glory, and to sense the angels and the saints.

The other things follow. Evangelism, teaching, fellowship, and much more, do indeed happen in the Eucharist,
but not because we set out to do them. They happen
because the worship is pure and deep and filled with the
Spirit. People are converted, people are taught, people
are drawn together, but only if they are touched by the
power of the worship, and that depends on the
relationship of the community to God. It is a kind of
turning on its head that is part of the divine way of
things. It works something like this.

We offer to God our worship, as much in Spirit and in
truth as we can. In our deluded human way we imagine
it to be worthy. In reality it falls far short of what it
ought to be, but God accepts it and uses it. We think we
are giving something to him and, lo and behold, he turns
it round and makes of it a gift to us. We have brought
him our worship; he has turned it into a tool of
evangelism or teaching or fellowship. That is his activity,
not ours. We offer the worship; he does the rest. Not
surprising perhaps in a sacrament where we bring bread
and wine, and here again find them returned to us
changed by his touch. He turns our offering into gift.
Such is his way.

Bread for the world

There is a danger in stressing how we must stretch up to
God if in doing so we put all the emphasis on our human
initiative. The truth is that we have a God who stretches
down to us. Indeed one of the marvels of the Eucharist,
one of the reasons why it is so satisfying a form of
worship, is that we have no sooner lifted hearts and
hands to symbolize our desire to be in heaven than we
are celebrating a God who in a very special sense has
come among us. Although Christians will never entirely
agree about how they understand that presence in the
Eucharist, the truth that 'The Lord is here', as thanks is

given over bread and wine and as they are shared, is one in which all can rejoice. So it is one of the paradoxes of our faith that at the very point that we reach up to heaven we are reminded that ours is a God who in Christ is very much on the earth. This is not contradiction, only paradox, and in a paradox you need to hold on to both truths.

We need to guard against a churchiness that excludes the world from our worship, and especially from the Eucharist. We sometimes make it a hopelessly churchy affair; we can almost believe that is the way it has got to be. But the Eucharist is full of the world. There is penitence, and when we have penitence as part of public liturgy it is a recognition of the corporate nature of human sin. There is intercession, and at their best the prayers of the Eucharist are broad in their concerns and sympathies, and become a lifting up to the Father of the whole of his creation. There is bread and wine and, for all their specific Christian symbolism, these are universal human symbols of life and work and leisure. There is the cross, there is the blood shed for all for the forgiveness of sins, there is the Lamb of God who takes away the sins of the world and grants peace. We should be suspicious of being 'sent out into the world', for the Eucharist is set in the world and proclaims the world's salvation.

All this leads us to take the Eucharist with utmost seriousness, never to celebrate it without a yearning to be joined to heaven, never to celebrate it without a vision of a world redeemed, and never to celebrate it without ensuring that it is, at a whole series of levels, a lively sacrifice. That will mean care for the detail, as well as openness to the Spirit.

Part II

2

PEOPLE AND PRAYER

The congregation

It is easy to say that every Eucharist should be a reaching up to heaven to share the worship of the angels. It is more difficult to see how this comes about. I believe that the key lies in understanding the role of the people, the congregation, in the Eucharist. It is the congregation's participation that is crucial, and we very easily misunderstand what that participation is.

The word 'congregation' needs rescuing before we can go any further. Rightly understood, it is a description of the whole assembly gathered for worship, all the lay people together with their ministers. There is nobody participating in the celebration who is not a member of the congregation. It is a wonderfully inclusive term. We have turned it into quite the opposite. We have taken out the ordained ministers, and so can use a phrase like 'the minister turns to the congregation'. We have, very often, taken out the choir, and thus we can have settings of the Eucharist written 'for choir and congregation'. 'Congregation' has become a description of those who have no other role, the passive receivers, those down there in the nave. This is a dreadful debasement.

Perhaps the word is beyond redemption. The Roman Catholic Church speaks instead of the 'assembly' in order to regain the sense of the whole community gathered. But it would seem a pity to let 'congregation' go, for it is a word in our Anglican vocabulary, and if we could recover its meaning, a very important lesson would be learnt. The congregation is the whole assembly. The worshippers come, in all their variety, individual people with their own needs and expectations, but as the liturgy begins they become a congregation. They discover their corporate identity as they give glory to God who is the Father of them all. The key to true worship is that participation of the whole congregation.

Yet the word 'participation' also needs rescuing. It was seen as one of the great benefits of the new rites in the 1960s and 1970s that they allowed for far greater participation than the Prayer Book Communion rite or the old Roman Mass, in which the people could seem very passive. It was not just that they remained kneeling, for most of the service, in their pews, but that their vocal participation was very limited also. In the Catholic tradition people spoke of 'hearing Mass', and that phrase summed up the problem.

Perhaps it was therefore inevitable that 'participation' should become the watchword, and be understood in a rather superficial way. For many churches it could be described as 'everyone joining in everything possible'. Some clergy have missed no opportunity to invite the people to say words with them, whether it be the 'set' parts of the Intercession, or the introduction to the Peace, or even whole paragraphs of the Eucharistic Prayer. The effect is disastrous. Words written for speaking by a single voice become heavy and turgid when ploughed through together. Opportunity for slight variation to pick up the mood and season of the day is lost when all are reciting in unison, and so 'set parts' become so set they might as well be in stone.

Vocal participation is at its best in dialogue. The opening of the Eucharistic Prayer illustrates this:

> The Lord is here.
> **His Spirit is with us**.
> Lift up your hearts.
> **We lift them to the Lord**.
> Let us give thanks to the Lord our God.
> **It is right to give him thanks and praise**.

Spoken with clarity and feeling it provides a momentum to the prayer that is carried on through the parts spoken by the president alone, to which the people respond at points in the *Sanctus*, Acclamation, and doxology. Where there is felt to be a need, more responses by the people can be part of the prayer, but the words put into their mouths need to be words written for speaking in chorus, not words for a single voice. Some of the shorter prayers in the new rites (though not the Eucharistic Prayers themselves) are written to be said together. It remains true that participation is not about everybody saying everything.

In other church communities participation has been seen mainly in terms of singling people out for particular ministries that together make up the whole. This is getting closer to the truth, and indeed there is something very important here that will be examined later in this chapter. But even this understanding has its difficulty, for, if participation means coming out of your pew to do something 'up front', whether singing, or reading, or nowadays even dancing, there is a danger that those who have none of those gifts, and who will always stay within the security of the pew, will feel excluded. Apparently worship means using a liturgical gift, and they are apparently liturgically ungifted.

To discover true participation we must look for something in which *all* may share. I suspect that it is that person in the pew, who is possibly the most reticent member of the congregation, who can provide the clue. For, in the end, I believe that the deepest level of congregational participation is *praying* the liturgy. The most active and crucial contribution may be the one that, to the outsider, may seem a passive non-role. We may be participating most deeply when we are silent and still.

Praying the liturgy

What is needed is a kind of undercurrent of prayerfulness that sustains the worship from opening greeting to concluding Dismissal and which comes to the surface,

so to speak, at those moments in the liturgy that are
specifically labelled 'Prayer'.

The classic opening stages to eucharistic worship
(admittedly long-lost and only just being recovered – see
Chapter 9 for a more detailed discussion) is the
president's greeting and the invitation 'Let us pray', a
time of silent corporate prayer, and then the drawing
together of that prayer in the Collect.

The classic form of the Prayers of the Faithful (again
long lost, but being recovered in some of today's forms
of Intercession – see Chapter 12) is a repeated sequence
consisting of biddings by the deacon, silent prayer by
the people, and collect by the president.

One of the options for the end of the Eucharist is
corporate silent prayer emerging, so to speak, from the
sharing of communion, and rounded off by a presidential
collect before the Dismissal.

In all three of these examples, it is clear that the
prayer is the people's task. Deacons or other ministers
may set the agenda for that prayer in biddings, and
presidents may draw the prayer to a close in a collect,
but the praying is by the whole community and very
often it is when all are silent. This is very far removed
from much of our liturgical praying in the Church of
England, which is the relentless pouring out of words,
either by the whole congregation, or more often by a
single leader, who proceeds without pause, let alone
genuine space for silence, with the people trying to keep
up with the leader's thoughts, and responding with an
'Amen' to make it their own.

I suspect that the first stage towards the recovery of
this concept of praying the liturgy is to concentrate on
those particular points in the service, and to work away
at making them genuine moments of deepening prayerfulness by the whole congregation. We need to help
people to rediscover the classic 'Let us pray' as an
invitation to do just that, to engage with the living God,
rather than as an instruction to change posture. The use
of 'Let us pray' to mean 'Please kneel down' has deprived

this little invitation of its straightforward but crucial meaning, and, as with 'congregation' and 'participation', if we can communicate what it really means, we shall teach a valuable lesson.

If we can show people how to pray at these key stages in worship, and to see that prayer as being of the very essence of the liturgy, and if we can show them how to use silence creatively, then I believe that a new attitude of mind will develop that will begin to affect the whole service. Prayer may only be on the surface at certain moments, but it goes underground still flowing, through the other activities of the Eucharist, so that all of them are carried along in prayer. This prayer may be unconscious, but everything is being approached with prayerfulness.

We hear the Scriptures read, but in a way we *pray* them; and that is why God is able to speak to us through them. We listen to the sermon, but in a way we *pray* it, and it is partly the prayer that changes it from dry theology into good news for our lives. We sing hymns and psalms, canticles and choruses, but at another level we *pray* them. St Augustine is credited with the view that those who sing pray twice. For many people we need to recover the sense that those who sing are praying at all. We tend to compartmentalize our worship, and not to see the thread of praying running through it all. We offer our hand to others at the Greeting of Peace, but if we want that to be something that expresses and deepens the Body of Christ, we have to *pray* that peacemaking; and if we do, it will no doubt change the way the Greeting of Peace looks as it is shared among us. We come to the altar table to receive, but we do not leave our prayers behind in our pew, but bring them with us and *pray* ourselves through the reception of the bread and wine. At every point, whatever is going on at the surface, the liturgy is being prayed. That under-standing of prayer shared and practised is a key to the renewal of worship.

I think that part of what some people value in the

Prayer Book tradition is the ability to submerge oneself in totally familiar and unchanging words, setting one free to pray at another level. It is one of the ironies of the Anglican '8 o'clock' tradition that you habitually took with you to church your copy of the Prayer Book, though you had no need of it because you knew the service off by heart. You opened it probably at the Epistle and Gospel, and followed them, but otherwise you did not use it. It is easy to see how that could and did produce services that were stale and barren. But it didn't, and doesn't, have to be so, and there is an important lesson to be learnt by those who prepare worship. We need to be set free, at least some of the time, from the printed page and reading to keep up, if our praying is not to be a terrible struggle.

I am conscious of the danger that praying the liturgy can easily degenerate into doing one's private thing in worship. Even that cannot always be wrong, and there ought not to be too much guilt where the worship has set us free to think our own thoughts. Nevertheless praying the liturgy is different from using it as a setting for personal devotion. Some in earlier generations were brought up to take to church, not the Book of Common Prayer, but the particular devotional manual given them at their confirmation. Often it provided them with a prayer for every gap in the service, and that could constitute praying the liturgy, but on the whole the prayers were too formal and also too personal to fulfil that function. They encouraged the worshipper to withdraw into a private world of 'me and God', and did not foster the sense of corporate worship and identity. That style has gone out of fashion, replaced by an emphasis on the worshipper being caught up in the central shared action of the service. That is almost wholly good, for what is needed is not a return to an individualistic piety. But something of that spirit of prayer, albeit in a new more spontaneous form that is always conscious that we pray *together*, needs rescuing, probably through teaching and trying and reflecting together in the parish, rather than through the issuing of a new wave of little holy books.

The use of silence

Progress down this path to a more prayerful liturgy cannot be made without a new and bold use of silence in our worship. It is not easy, for in many churches it has had no part at all in worship for generations. Some are threatened by it. Some clergy are sure their people cannot cope with it. Some churchpeople suspect it is the vicar who cannot cope with it, and yearn for the space it provides. We live therefore in a transitional era when it may be necessary to help people rather self-consciously to use the silence well, in a way that one hopes would not be necessary when the skill has been acquired. For it is a skill, and not one that comes naturally to everyone, though everyone can benefit from it once acquired.

A few ground rules may help.

Silence must be for everyone (except just occasionally the musicians – see Chapter 22). If silence appears to be simply because the people are waiting for the ministers to finish some task (cleansing the vessels after communion, for instance), the conclusion will inevitably be drawn that silence is merely because we are not yet ready to go on. If silence is to be taken seriously, everyone, ministers in the sanctuary included, need to be still and seen to be part of it.

Silences need to be of the right length. One cannot prescribe how long. It will depend on the type of service, the kind of congregation, the experience of silence the people have, and much else. But, as a general rule, a distinction needs to be drawn between the kind of momentary silence, that enables an idea to be assimilated, and a more extended silence, in which people can *develop* thoughts and prayers.

The silence before the confession is likely, at ordinary celebrations, to be of the first sort, just enough time for people to call to mind particular things they want to bring to the prayers of penitence, and to recollect themselves before joining in the corporate words. Silence after readings may come in the same category, pause for thought, before moving on. These are not invariable rules. There will be occasions when the silence at these two points could be longer, but probably not normally so. On the other hand, the silence after the distribution may be the point for a longer communal silence, which in a mature congregation might be of two or three minutes.

There is a question of posture. Those momentary silences can be sustained whether the congregation is standing, kneeling or sitting. Before the confession the people may well be standing, after the reading they may be sitting, after the Eucharistic Prayer kneeling. If the silence is short it does not matter much. But, if the silence is of the longer sort, with real space to reflect and to develop prayer, standing will nearly always be inappropriate, and kneeling a strain for some. Sitting will probably be best, and it needs the ministers to be seated too, and not be hovering over the altar, looking as if they are about to get on with the next thing.

Silence is good, but too much silence destroys the momentum of the liturgy. A minister and a community need to be selective about the points where they opt for silence, especially of the longer sort. Where a pause becomes a break, people can lose the development of the service. The tradition recognizes the need to draw people together at the conclusion of silence; this is the strength of the Collect.

There is also the need to have some kind of distinction between silence for reflection and silence for prayer. They are not two entirely different things, for the one should lead naturally into the other. But silence before the Collect is clearly for corporate prayer, whereas silence after the reading is to reflect upon what has been heard. If people are at any early stage in their use of silence in worship, they are helped by instructions that say, not so much 'Silence is kept', as 'Let us pray silently for a few minutes', or 'Let us reflect in silence on what we have heard'. Simply to be plunged into silence unbidden makes it more difficult to know how to use that time.

Silent prayer by the congregation does not necessarily mean no sound in the building. It is important that we learn to treasure that total silence, when one can hear a pin drop, but silent prayer can be offered as music is played or sung. Some of the frustration of those who complain of choir anthems as 'performances' would disappear if people could learn to pray the anthem, to see it as stimulus to prayer, and if the choir understood what they were providing. Here is another skill at which we need to work.

All with their ministry

Providing that we are clear about the primary expression of participation in the Eucharist through this prayerful attentiveness, we can return to look positively at the secondary level of participation of which mention was made earlier, through being called out of the congregation to exercise a particular skill or ministry.

In most churches we have moved on from the days when one man (and it was always a man, never a woman) dominated the service, reserving the spoken parts almost entirely to himself, perhaps delegating a reading (almost inevitably to another man). In a great many churches a wide cross-section of men, women and children take their turn in reading the Scriptures, in leading prayers, and in other vocal parts of the service. Indeed the problem in some church communities is that too many people are drawn out to do this in a single service, without much sense of anyone being in charge, and the service loses its cohesion (and more about this in the following chapter).

People are also learning that this move to wider participation at this level is not a purely practical thing, but has a theological base. They are understanding that the passage about gifts in 1 Corinthians 12 and the passage about ministries in Ephesians 4 point to a pattern of church life where this is appropriate. If we want to express and symbolize the nature of the Body of Christ, we want to do it in worship, and supremely when we share in a liturgy that is itself a reflection on the meaning of the Body of Christ. The Eucharist both forms and reflects the Church. In other words, on the one hand, because we organize Christian worship as a co-operative venture in which all contribute their gifts to help build up and sustain the whole, the Church is helped to become that all the more. Yet, on the other hand, because the Church is like that already, it is natural that when we come to worship we should give expression to it ritually.

I believe it to be important to make a distinction between the gifts we exercise in the liturgy and the gifts we use in daily life both in the Church and in the wider community. It is not that some people have churchy gifts, and exercise their ministry mainly on Sundays and mainly in sanctuaries and sacristies, while others have gifts more appropriate to the world outside. It does look like that sometimes in churches, where some of those keenest to be employed in the liturgy seem least happy to get involved where the Church is most engaged with daily life. The truth surely is that God gives us *all* gifts to use in daily life, whether we exercise them chiefly through the Church's direct work or whether we exercise them chiefly at home, or at work, or in wider secular community concerns. But, additionally, the Church then invites us *all* to have a share, a particular ministry, in worship, so that we express ritually in worship that mutual dependence that we have in daily life.

Sometimes the ritual ministry we have in church is a natural extension of the gift we are using day by day. A teacher reads the lesson in church. A person whose daily work is keeping a home clean, tidy and welcoming gives an afternoon to making the church building the same. But it need not always be so. The nurse may sing in the choir, the sales manager may look after the churchyard. The liturgical ministry is simply revealing something about the way the Body of Christ functions, though there is a special appropriateness where it reflects a God-given gift and skill.

We have noted already the difficulty with making too much of the need for every one to have a ministry – 'every member ministry' – in liturgy as well as in wider church life. It can exclude. It can make it appear that to be part of the Body you need to have a gift, and some feel ungifted. The problem arises if we have too narrow a view of what constitutes a liturgical ministry. If we restrict it to those who distribute holy communion, lead prayers and read lessons, we have taken the narrow view. Perhaps most people would broaden it very naturally to include those who welcome at the door, those who take the collection and bring up the bread and wine, those who serve and those who sing in the choir. That is less exclusive, but still it makes liturgical ministry a minority activity in most churches. We need to broaden it further. Every work that contributes to the spirit, the beauty and the smooth-running of worship is a liturgical ministry. Those who at the service sit in their pew, but who in the days and hours before have washed the linen, arranged the flowers, typed the service sheet, or rung the bells, have made their contribution too. And, if we may broaden it one stage further, the person whose only gift is to bring a deeper commitment to maintain that undercurrent of prayer than most can bring has possibly brought the most precious thing of all.

Yes, participation may indeed be about everyone exercising a ministry, but there are more ministries that contribute to the whole than most imagine. That is true, of course, not only in the liturgy, but in daily living too, and is a truth not to be lost in either setting.

We should not exaggerate the novelty of all this. People may not have articulated it quite like this in the past, but the idea was present. In particular the ministry of the organist and the choir has always been recognized, though not always as part of the congregation (see Chapter 22). The presence in the chancel and the sanctuary of men (and sometimes women) as assistants and servers of different kinds, has always been a ministry, at least in theory, of representatives of the people, the whole congregation, so that there are lay people, not just ordained ministers, in the drama as it unfolds. Yet, although that has been the theory, very often choir and servers have not seemed like representatives of the people, but more like a different order of ministry altogether.

One of the ways in which we exalt some ministries at the expense of others is the way that we authorize people for ministries. A lay person needs the bishop's authorization to help with the distribution of holy communion, but not to read the Scriptures in the liturgy. In many parishes those who are to sing are admitted to the choir during public worship. Those who arrange the flowers are not. Inevitably some ministries are affirmed and some are not. Baptism is the commission to minister within the Body of Christ; commissionings should be used sparingly and, when they are used, perhaps they could be related to that baptismal calling.

Some particular ministries

Although there should be no hierarchy of ministries, there are some ministries in the Eucharist about which a little more needs to be said.

First, there is the man or woman authorized to help

with the distribution of holy communion. Permission to do this is normally nowadays given to men and women alike, as permission to distribute the consecrated bread as much as to deliver the cup, and, in many places, that permission extends from the church to the homes of the housebound when the sacrament it taken to them by extended Communion (see Chapter 16). In some ways it is unfortunate that this ministry needs a kind of episcopal permission that makes it different from others. It tends to mean that fewer people share in this ministry than could do so, and that, where the diocese allows permission to be renewed, those who exercise it tend to keep it, almost as a job for life, and can become 'clericalized' through the process.

There is nothing priestly about the distribution of the consecrated elements. However much we may hold to ordained presidency of the rite, there is absolutely no doctrinal reason why lay people should not exercise this role, and, even for those who question most seriously the ordination of women as priests, no reason why a woman should not do so.

It is a task that needs to be done well. At the moment of communion, people do not want to meet with a lack of assurance that draws attention to the individual. So it is a ministry for which people need careful preparation and practice, and a ministry that people need to exercise sufficiently regularly to become confident about it. (The question of dress for communion assistants and other ministers in the sanctuary is discussed in Chapter 8.)

Another group around the altar are the servers. Some churches do without them. Some have a faithful one or two. Quite common practice is three: crucifer and two acolytes. Some have an army of them, and find a job for all. The motive for having them is sometimes pastoral, rather than liturgical. How do we hold the youngsters in the church? Give them a job to do! It is not a bad principle. Many priests and deacons today found their vocation in the proximity to holy things that serving involves.

But there are other considerations as well as the pastoral. The number of servers ought to be dictated at least in part by the liturgical space in which they operate. In a small chancel and sanctuary too many bodies falling over one another can detract from the liturgy. Worship is never served by fussiness. There is, in any case, a good argument for not having a job for everybody every week, for, if these ministries are representative ones called out of the midst of the congregation, there ought to be the discipline that those who are sometimes in the sanctuary are also sometimes in the pew. If we cannot hold our youngsters without a job to do every week, we need to look at our church life and liturgy, rather than at our serving rota.

Even if it is for pastoral reasons that we first draw people in as servers, we need then to make them liturgically competent. Some will always be more graceful than others, and some will always look rather out of place in the sanctuary – and that may witness to something important. But they should be trained to be as competent as they can. It isn't sufficient to dress them up and shove a candle in their hand.

They need to be competent for their own self-esteem and sense of achievement. They need to be competent because incompetence draws attention to itself and distracts the worshipper.

They need to be competent because they are there to enable things to run more smoothly and to remove from the president those things about which he should not need to worry. If, through their incompetence, instead of being relieved of concerns, he takes on board the extra worry of his servers and their extraordinary ways, his own ability to enter into his own very sensitive and demanding role is threatened.

Finally, if it is not a cliché, they need to be competent, because God deserves only the best, and it is he, more than the priest or the people, who is being served.

A further group of ministers are the 'readers'. We use that word confusedly in the Church of England to mean both those authorized lay people who may preach and lead worship ('lay readers' as we often, if technically incorrectly, call them) and also ordinary members of the congregation coming to the lectern to read the Scriptures. I am here referring to this latter category (though the former, 'lay readers', are discussed in the following chapter).

There is a tradition that the reading of the Gospel at the Eucharist is the prerogative of the deacon (and who should read the Gospel is discussed in Chapter 11). But, with that possible exception, the reading of the Scriptures is not a ministry reserved to clergy. In the old High Mass ritual of the Catholic tradition the Epistle was read by the subdeacon, and the subdeacon was a member of a lay, not an ordained, order, and his equivalent in today's church is a lay person, male or female, not a priest. The Old Testament reading also is part of the laity's ministry. It should not, in general, be usurped by the clergy, however many of them there are present.

What is being said about the nature of the Church at the ordination of a bishop when the Bishop of London reads the Gospel, the Bishop of Winchester the Epistle, and the dean of the cathedral the Old Testament reading? It suggests hierarchy, and ordained hierarchy at that. It implies that lay people read the Scriptures in the liturgy, not by right, but by default when there is no one more important to do so.

Similarly the Prayers of Intercession are 'The Prayers of the Faithful', the people's prayers. Traditionally the deacon has a hand in them (drawing them into shape and order as part of a ministry of serving the people), but they are the people's prayers, and again should not be taken over entirely by the clergy (see Chapters 3 and 12).

For both reading and leading prayer there should be adequate training. There will be occasions when a poor 'performance' is recognized as being acceptable, because for all its technical incompetence, it comes so clearly from the heart and is so filled with the Spirit. But, in general, we are asked to undertake particular ministries because, with training and practice, we are judged capable of doing them in such a way that the Body, and its worship, will be edified. There rests on every minister in charge of a church, and every worship committee, a responsibility to see that this training is given.

There is a final question, which some will think fanciful, about the balance in any celebration of the people who exercise representative ministries in chancel and sanctuary. It is not a question that would have been asked a generation ago, at least not in relation to gender. The ministers would all have been male from priest to smallest server. But what do we say about the nature of the Church if the whole team leading worship – clergy, servers, readers, communion assistants and the like – is male, or female, or old, or young? If the liturgy is a kind of acting out of the life of the Church, should we not, without being silly about it, try to ensure that there is a good mixture in every celebration? Do we not by so doing affirm in a subtle way some categories of people who have felt excluded – whether it be women, or the young, or, in some churches, the old? We say something also, not only about the nature of the Church, but about the God who has broken down every barrier that divides us.

3

PRIEST AND DEACON

Presidency

Twenty years after its introduction into the liturgical rubrics of the Church of England, the term 'the president' at the Eucharist remains an unpopular description. It smacks too much of the secular world. It sounds new and of the twentieth century, though Justin Martyr spoke of 'him who presides over the brethren' in almost the first liturgical material we have outside the New Testament. It certainly sounds rather grand when it describes the priest at the weekday celebration with a congregation of three. People will prefer 'the celebrant', despite the truth that we are all celebrants at the Eucharist; or 'the minister', though we are all ministers of the gospel and the Eucharist has several liturgical ministers; or 'the priest', though even that has its theological problem for some.

Whether the term 'president' is used or not, the concept behind it is important, and every leader of worship needs to understand it. It applies not only to the Eucharist, though that is our concern here. It applies, equally, at some services where the president will not be a priest, but a deacon, a reader or another lay person. At its simplest it is about holding the congregation together.

It has a lot in common with the effective chairing of a meeting. I should not want to reduce the leadership of worship, let alone the exercise of Christian priesthood, to being about chairing a meeting, but that element is part of it.

How does a good chairman (or woman) function at a meeting? When the chairman is in place and calls for order, the meeting comes into being. He (or she) speaks at significant moments. A good chairman does not speak a great deal, but does ensure that the other contributions have balance and move the meeting forward. The chairman's own words include beginning the meeting and ending it, and certain other interventions, often expressed through an established formula: 'Are we now ready to vote on this?', 'I declare the motion carried', 'We will now move to next business.' On the whole these contributions are ones that draw the matters under discussion together, and sometimes draw the people together. Often they are contributions that would sound oddly out of place from the 'floor' of the meeting, but sound quite appropriate from the chairman. The good chairman does not stand throughout the meeting, dominating the assembly, but sits 'in the chair'; but the chair is always visible, and, if the chairman disappears from sight, the meeting is a little unsettled or uncertain. The chairman communicates with people not only through spoken interventions, but even with the smallest gesture of hand or eye to restrain, to encourage or to reassure. The good chairman has a clear idea about how the meeting should go, how it might develop, and even when it might end.

The leadership of Christian worship will include much more than that, but it is difficult to see that much of that is irrelevant to good liturgical presidency. Worship can be impaired both by over-strong presidency that dominates, and by a lack of presidency, in which there is little sense that anyone is holding the assembly together, or that it is going anywhere.

The rubrics of Holy Communion Rite A (and indeed of the other eucharistic rites of the Church of England) are designed to give the service a proper sense of presidency. On page 115 of The Alternative Service Book, note 2 says this:

The president (who, in accordance with the provisions of Canon B12 'Of the ministry of the Holy Communion', must have been episcopally ordained priest) presides over the whole service. He says the opening Greeting, the Collect, the Absolution, the Peace, and the Blessing; he himself must take the bread and the cup before replacing them on the holy table, say the Eucharistic Prayer, break the consecrated bread, and receive the sacrament on every occasion. The remaining parts of the service he may delegate to others.

The issue here is not principally about priesthood (and who may absolve, consecrate, bless, etc.), but about presidency. The particular words and actions that are reserved to the president are exactly those parts that need to be the prerogative of the representative figure who holds the community together. They are the equivalent of the chairman's words at a meeting which 'include beginning and ending it' and are the contributions 'that draw the matters under discussion together, and sometimes draw the people together', the contributions 'that sound oddly out of place from the floor of the meeting'.

If people need a basic sense of security in which to be open to change and surprise, part of that security comes through a good experience of presidency. Like so much else in liturgy, people may not talk in such terms, but they know when a service has been badly led and when there has been no sense of leadership at all. The more people who have a distinctive 'up front' part in the liturgy, reading, leading prayers and so on, the stronger the need for a sense of one who presides.

The kind of profile that presidency requires will also differ from community to community and occasion to occasion. There are celebrations of the Eucharist, where everybody knows what they are doing and where the service is going, where there needs to be only the lightest touch from a leader. There are other times when, either because there are people present not accustomed to worshipping together, or because there are to be unfamiliar elements in the service, a far higher profile presidency is needed. Leaders of worship need to become sensitive to this.

The Rite A note quoted above provides a good outline

of the president's speaking role. It leaves a good deal to
be delegated, and it allows also for the development of a
second, complementary, minister's role, and this we
shall look at in the liturgical ministry of the deacon.
There are not many circumstances where pastoral
considerations should lead to setting that note aside. In
particular the delegating of the leadership of the first
half of the service to a deacon, reader or other lay
person, is unfortunate, theologically and liturgically,
both because the concept of overall presidency of the rite
is lost, and also because the unity of word and sacrament
which the Eucharist proclaims so strongly is undermined. Where it is desirable to develop a second
ministry, the model is that of the president/deacon
relationship, not a kind of co-presidency or serial
presidency as the rite develops.

But of course presidency, like good chairmanship, is
about much besides words that are spoken. It is about
visibility, posture and seating (and Chapter 4 looks at
this), and it is about even the smallest gesture of hand
and eye (see Chapter 5). Putting all these things together,
presidency can be seen to be about bringing and holding
the worshipping community together, providing it with
a focus, being a kind of anchor, and thus giving it the
security in which to be free.

It has its own danger, for the focus that the president
wants to provide is to draw people to Christ who, at a
deeper level, presides among his people. There is a style
of presidency that draws people to the priest, and there
is a theology that gives respectability to that. But Christ
is found in the Eucharist in the assembly, the people
who come together and become his Body, rather than in
one individual. The danger is there in the current
practice, good in every other way, of the priest facing the
people over the altar table; it gives him a Christ role that
in the Anglican tradition has rarely been expressed
before. The president has to draw together and hold
together, but not in order that the congregation may be
his, but that it may be Christ's.

One of the things at which the president therefore needs to work is the right use of his own personal qualities and characteristics. There are clergy who were trained to exclude everything of themselves in the celebration of the Eucharist. As far as humanly possible, they left their individual personalities in the vestry as they put on the anonymous vestments of priesthood, and in the celebration played down the gestures of face and eye and hand, and the kind of personal words, that communicated something of themselves. All that for the best of reasons, so that it should be Christ who was proclaimed, not themselves. Yet we can only communicate our faith, our affection and joy in Christ by being ourselves.

For some the problem, if they recognize it, is the opposite one. They have grown so used to communicating the power of Christ through the attractiveness of their own personalities that they cannot see that Christ is obscured, and they are drawing people, not to him, but to themselves. In gesture and in word, the minister must be himself (or herself), but very often with a proper restraint, and never more so than when presiding at the Eucharist.

Part of the way in which the president ensures that it is around Christ that the people are being drawn is in the *prayerfulness* he brings to the celebration. Here clergy often encounter a problem. They sometimes speak with appreciation of their rare Sunday off as the opportunity to be able to worship, as if the business of enabling other people to do so meant one had to forfeit the opportunity oneself. But a minister who can enter at a deep level into an experience of worship only on three or four Sundays a year, and those probably away from his or her own community, has little chance of seeing the congregation deepening its corporate spirituality. If the minister is to be a person of prayer, he or she must above all else be a person at prayer at the liturgy. If there is a need to recover for the whole congregation the sense of 'praying the liturgy', there is a need just as much for clergy and others who lead worship to believe that they can preside and pray at one and the same time.

The delegating of parts of the worship to others not only affirms something important about the nature of the Body of Christ, but also sets the president free to be at prayer during the service. The role of the deacon helps him here. By this or other means he needs to ask, 'How can I set myself free of worry about detail so that I can pray myself and these people through the liturgy?' Part of the answer will be in the preparation that needs to go into every service, but that is not the whole answer. During the service itself the president needs to be sufficiently unencumbered with detail to be free to be at prayer.

The Deacon

The tradition of the Church gives us a second complementary role of leadership in the Eucharist, that of the deacon. It is difficult to discuss this role in the Church of England just at the present, because the idea of the deacon's ministry is confused by the issue of the ordination of women to the priesthood. At present there are many women, who feel their calling is to the priesthood, who are nevertheless exercising their ministry within the order of deacons. What I want to describe here is not something to provide some sort of liturgical ministry for women deacons to alleviate the pain of being denied the priesthood, but a ministry that benefits the Church, enhances the Eucharist, and can be exercised by men as well as women. Indeed I think it is important that those who preside at the Eucharist should sometimes also fulfil the complementary role of deacon.

What emerges from the tradition as the role of the deacon at the Eucharist is a list of possible duties like this:

The deacon —
    is the president's 'right-hand person';
    proclaims the gospel reading;

takes his or her turn in preaching
invites the congregation – to confess, to exchange the
    Peace, to make an Acclamation, etc;
organizes the Prayers of Intercession;
prepares the altar table for the celebration;
shares in the breaking of the bread and the distribution
    of the bread and wine;
gives practical instructions – about posture, page
    numbers, etc.;
dismisses the people at the end.

Not all of this will be appropriate in every setting. On
the other hand there are other tasks that may be assigned
to the deacon, not listed here, some of them depending
on the kind of ritual that a church employs. None of
those listed here conflict with the ASB Rite A's note
about presidency, though in the actual text of the service
the Dismissal, traditionally part of the deacon's ministry,
is assigned to the president. More recent service books
have not followed the ASB in this respect.

What lie behind this list are two main assumptions
about the deacon's role.

The first is that it is a ministry that makes explicit the
element of service that lies hidden in all ministries. The
deacon serves God in serving both the congregation and
the president. The members of the congregation are
served by the way the deacon encourages them and
helps them through the service. All through the deacon
is inviting them to do things, and making it easier for
them to do so. But the president is also served by being
relieved of some tasks and assisted with other tasks to
lighten his burden, and that is important if he is to be
free to be at prayer. Throughout the liturgy the deacon is
holding up to the priest and to the people a model of
service, a service that, though it is the deacon's particular
ministry, is one shared by the whole Church and by
every member of it, priest, deacon or lay person,
individually.

The second is that the ministry of the deacon, though
it is of service, is not of subservience. That is why it is

properly described as *complementary*. To the deacon is assigned the reading of the Gospel, the high point of the Liturgy of the Word. To the deacon is assigned the right to dismiss the assembly at the end. It is a two-person leadership of worship, a kind of team ministry, but one in which roles are clear. The two are not co-presidents, competing for a role, presiding from either end of the table like book-ends, or sitting on either side of the chancel knocking the service from one side to the other like a game of tennis. They belong together, they stand side by side, they support one another, and give way to one another, so that first one, and then the other, may move back into prayer, and then come forward to lead.

In the present state of the Church of England, this may mean that one of the two is always president and the other always deacon. That is not ideal, but a fully developed diaconal ministry at the Eucharist can be fulfilling to the woman who exercises it week by week, as well as a blessing to the president and the people. What would say much more about the nature of Christian ministry is where two people, both in priest's orders (but also therefore both in deacon's orders) alternated in the role they fulfilled at the Eucharist. The recovery of the role of the deacon at the Eucharist may lead eventually to this norm in any church where more than one ordained minister serves.

The same ASB note already discussed adds,

> When necessity dictates, a deacon or lay person may preside over the Ministry of the Word.

The only necessity that would normally dictate would be the absence of a priest. A deacon then presides over a curtailed rite, and needs then to take on board all that has been said about presidency.

The Reader

Mention has already been made of the office of Reader, and how the reader is to exercise a liturgical ministry. In a church where eucharistic worship is the norm, this can be a puzzle. Of course the reader may take his or her turn in preaching, and may share in the distribution of bread and wine. But those who have been trained and licensed as readers often have gifts and skills in leading worship. The temptation for the parish priest, especially if he wants to affirm the reader's ministry, is, despite the rubric above, to hand over the first part of the Eucharist to the reader and to introduce a dual presidency to the rite. As with the deacon, this is hardly ever the right solution, and certainly outside what is permitted.

My own belief is that the deacon's role provides the proper model for the reader's liturgical ministry at the Eucharist. Indeed the way the Church of England has developed the work readers do means that they are deacons in all but name and ordination. There are those who would want to make a distinction in what they delegate to deacons and to readers, but, on the whole, if the case is well made for a second and complementary ministry in the Eucharist, alongside that of the president, it will be helpful to the priest, who has no one in deacon's orders upon whom to call, to develop the ministry of the reader in this way. What has been set out in the section above would then apply almost entirely to the reader.

The argument can be taken one step further. If it is to the benefit of the Church that there be a second diaconal minister at the Eucharist, in parishes where there is no deacon and no reader, should the parish priest train suitable men and women to be the deacon of the Eucharist, even without the grace of orders, so that he, like other presidents in other churches, may be set free from the detail to concern himself with the prayerful bringing of the people to Christ in worship? My own answer would be Yes, for the whole Church does share the *diakonia*, but I would want to ensure that a variety of people shared this ministry, rather than that it should become the prerogative of one or two.

Concelebration?

Any discussion of the practice of 'concelebration' will be
foreign to many parts of the Church, and particularly to
Evangelicals, and there will be a suspicion that it smacks
of the worst sort of clericalism. In the theology of the
Church of England's eucharistic rites, the only real
meaning of the term 'concelebration' would be that every
Eucharist is a concelebration and every communicant a
concelebrant, and indeed the word 'concelebration' has
no place in either Prayer Book or ASB. The nearest we
come to it is in a note at Ordinations that 'it is
appropriate that the newly ordained should be invited
by the bishop to exercise their new ministry in the
course of the service'. In the Roman practice, which is
where the fashion has sprung from, concelebration
means that all the priests present who concelebrate
share among them some of the presidential or diaconal
functions, and at the time of the Eucharistic Prayer
gather around the altar, with the presiding celebrant,
share in some of his gestures, and recite together the
narrative of the institution, though the voice of the
president is always to remain firmly leading. In addition
some paragraphs of the Eucharistic Prayer may be
delegated to a concelebrant.

The Church of England's Liturgical Commission, in a
1982 report, made a distinction between this Roman
practice, which it labelled 'co-consecration' and which it
deprecated, and 'ritual concelebration', which it thought
permissible. By ritual concelebration it meant that other
priests might gather around the president at the altar,
and maybe share some of his gestures, but leave him
alone to recite the words of the Eucharistic Prayer.
Ritual concelebration becomes, in a sense, a ceremonial
detail, often decided by questions of setting and space.
A good case can be made for it, where the relationship
and unity of that particular group of clergy is to be
affirmed. A team of priests, a cathedral chapter for
instance, who work together might, on some occasions,
affirm something about their shared ministry by being

grouped together around the altar. A bishop might also, wherever he went in his diocese, have his priests grouped around him at the altar to say something about the ministry they share with him. But it should always be in such a way that a more fundamental truth, about the unity and relationship of the whole congregation, is affirmed.

For that is the function of priests and deacons in the Eucharist. They have a special expertise in liturgy and a special role to perform, but the offering of the worship of the Church is not the private domain of one order, but the activity of the whole community. It is that whole community, among whom president and deacon minister, that needs to feel that it is celebrating the Holy Eucharist.

4

FURNISHINGS AND SPACE

The focus of the word

The principal furnishings of a church are never simply for practical use, though they do need to be that. There are three such principal furnishings: the font or baptistry, which is a permanent sign of entry and of baptism; the lectern or pulpit, which is a permanent sign of the significance of the word of God in Scripture; and the altar or holy table, which is a permanent sign of the eucharistic meal. There are other furnishings, but they do not carry the same symbolic significance as these three. Thus word and sacrament (through the two dominical sacraments of baptism and Eucharist) have equal place and honour, and each should stand out in the church with its own space and dignity, and in proportion to one another.

The font is not the immediate concern of this book (but see Chapter 20), but both the focus of word and that of meal are important.

The English parish church, conformed to Victorian fashion, has, as the focus of the word, both lectern and pulpit on either side of the chancel step, standing for two aspects of the place of Scripture in the liturgy, the lectern for reading and the pulpit for preaching. In contrast, many newer churches have just the one, normally a simple lectern, serving for both reading and preaching. In the Roman Church, a single furnishing, normally more significant than the simplest form of lectern, and called the ambo, serves for both. The Anglican 'three-decker pulpit' provided another example of the single focus.

There is of course a good deal to be said for this single

focus of the word at the Eucharist. All the Scriptures might be read at it and the sermon preached from it. Especially when the Scriptures are read from the same decent and large copy of the lectionary or Bible, something about the importance of Scripture, and the unity of this whole part of the liturgy, is affirmed. It is more effective than the kind of service where one reading is from a lectern, the Gospel from the midst of the nave, the sermon from the chancel step, and the pulpit is unused and ignored.

In an old church, where both lectern and pulpit exist, some choices need to be made. If both are decent and suitable furnishings, both ought to be employed. Despite what has just been said, there is nothing nonsensical in making a sub-division of the word between reading and preaching, lectern and pulpit. To leave one in place but unused during the liturgy is unfortunate. Nevertheless the lectern and pulpit may not be judged decent and suitable. In the case of the lectern, it may be in the form of a brass eagle on the top of an over-tall pedestal. It does not make for effective communication. In the case of the pulpit, it is often simply too high (and almost as often fairly simply lowered without destroying its form and proportion) or in the wrong place, obscuring the sanctuary and altar. With help from the Diocesan Advisory Committee it is normally possible to get good advice about which or both needs alteration, resiting or disposal after faculty.

However, the present fashion is sometimes to replace with something insubstantial. The brass eagle was at least a significant piece of furnishing. It suggested that the Bible that lay upon it was central to the Church and to its worship. The pulpit, even if it were too high, declared that preaching mattered. Where a new lectern or pulpit is to be introduced, or just one of these is to be retained, it needs to be a worthy enough piece of furnishing to continue to say that the Scriptures matter, that the preaching of the gospel matters, and it needs to be in proportion to the altar. We hold word and

sacrament in equal honour. Just as some of the Free
Churches have exalted the word over the sacrament in
their pulpit-dominated churches, with the holy table
dwarfed below the pulpit, we need to be wary of creating
the opposite imbalance, with the altar a solid and
sizeable furnishing and the lectern flimsy, insignificant,
and even carted away half way through the service. The
word must have an adequate focus, and that focus its
space around it.

The altar table

If the lectern or pulpit is the focus of the word part of
the Eucharist, the altar table is the focus for the meal
part, the gathering of the faithful to take bread and
wine, give thanks, break and share. The official service
books of the Church of England refer to the 'holy table',
out of deference to those who suspect in the word 'altar'
a hint of unacceptable doctrines about the Eucharist as
sacrifice. I am using the word 'altar' in this book, as well
as 'table', because it is the word commonly used by the
majority of Church of England people, and by it they –
and I – imply no narrow doctrinal position about which
anyone need worry.

The altar can be used in one of two ways. In some
churches, where it is well placed visually and very much
the dominant furnishing, perhaps with people on three,
if not four, sides, it will very naturally serve as the focal
point for the whole liturgy from beginning to end, and
the lectern or pulpit will simply be the place to which
people turn to hear the Scriptures read and the sermon
preached.

In other churches, either because the lectern or pulpit
is just as natural a focus as the altar, or because the
altar is in a difficult place, out of sight for some at least
of the congregation, and perhaps fixed against the wall,
it will be the focus only from the Eucharistic Prayer
onwards.

The ideal for modern liturgy is a free-standing altar,

with space on all sides of it, where the president may take his place behind it for the Eucharistic Prayer. There is a danger in this, mentioned in the previous chapter, of an over-identification of the president with Christ. Nevertheless, the sense of the community gathered in fellowship is greatly enhanced by this style of celebration, and it reflects some of the needs of our own day.

But people have been slow to work through some of the implications of a free-standing altar and a celebration facing the people. First of all the height and shape of the altar need to be questioned. Moving the existing altar away from the wall with no further change is not often satisfactory. Altars against the wall are often, in effect, sideboards, and sideboards are what one expects to find against walls. But sideboards are not naturally moved to be placed in the middle of the room. In the middle of a room one has a table, lower, deeper, probably nearer a square, depending of course on the shape of the room.

But, secondly, there are implications for almost every detail of the ritual of the Eucharist. What looks right, acted out with backs to the people against a wall, simply cannot be turned around with no further modifications.

The first implications are about posture and gesture. When the ministers had their backs to the people, kneeling at the altar was perfectly appropriate, and a genuflexion appeared a natural expression of reverence. But ministers kneeling or genuflecting behind the altar as they face the people look comical, and a diminutive eucharistic president with only his eyebrows and forehead peeping over the top of the table does not enhance a spirit of worship. The way the ministers use hands and arms in gesture needs to be rethought also (and these matters are considered in the following chapter).

There are implications, too, about what should be on the table.

With the sideboard altar and the ministers with their backs to the people obscuring what lay upon it, it was not too important how much was crowded on to the altar; and a great deal was. A cross, two or six candles, depending on taste, flower arrangements (except among the very high church), often a brass book stand, were in place all the time, and for the celebration of the Eucharist were added the vessels, covered at first with burse and veil, these later taken off, the one propped up like a cultic object and the other spread out to fill the only available gap. A few churches added framed cards with texts the priest might use, and, especially, when new texts began to appear, clergy often added an increasing number of little books to dip into and pairs of spectacles, with their cases, for every size of print.

But then the celebration was turned round to face the people. Some implications were recognized straight away. The cross had to be moved, often relocated on a shelf behind the altar. The flowers moved on to new pedestals, where ever larger and grander arrangements could develop. The candles on the table probably came down to two. But often that was as far as the rethinking went. The rest stayed and the congregation was exposed to the altar clutter.

The kind of simplification that goes with liturgical reform teaches us here that what needs to stand out on the holy table is bread and wine. They are what the eyes need to be drawn to. Anything that dwarfs them, anything that detracts from them and draws the eye to something else (the propped-up burse, for instance) is not serving the liturgy.

Bread and wine need to stand out during that part of the service when they are the focus, in other words from their preparation until they have been consumed. During that time the president's book needs to be at one side, so that they can be in the centre, the visual focus. He is at that point using the words in the service that change least and with which he is most familiar. Where the whole of the celebration is centred on the altar, if that is what the geography of the church dictates, the president will communicate with the people more effectively with his book in the centre, rather than to one side for the major part of the service. This is quite possible if the vessels remain at the credence table until they are needed.

In terms of focus, there is a particular question about cross and candles. The cross is not quite the focus during the eucharistic action that the bread and wine constitute, and yet it is not very far from being so, for they speak of the body broken and the blood shed on the cross. It is therefore appropriate that there should be a cross near the altar, though not necessarily behind it, where it can either be obscured by the president or look as if it is growing out of his head. Sometimes it hangs over the altar. Sometimes of course it is the cross that has been carried in procession at the entry of the ministers. For it ought not to be that a cross is used, rather like a verger's wand, to lead in the ministers, but that they bring in a cross and set it in a prominent place in the celebration. A cross that leads in and then disappears makes the wrong point. It follows that it is better to have one cross that becomes a significant part of the celebration, than a number of crosses – one behind the altar, one on the altar cloth, one processed in and attached to the choir stalls. That kind of superfluity undermines the power of the symbol and confuses the focus.

As for candles, Christians burn them to remind them of Christ who is our Light and the Light of all the world. For that reason they appropriately burn on or near the altar table, and especially near the bread and wine over which thanks are being given at the Eucharist, because altar and sacrament stand in a special sense for the presence of Christ the Light. It is equally appropriate that they burn near the place of the word, with the sense of illuminating the Scriptures, and again reminding us of Christ our Light who speaks to us through their pages. Whether the candles are on or only near the altar, whether they are part of the lectern or are brought to be near it, whether there are candles alight in the church before the service, or whether the only lights are those carried in by acolytes and brought in turn to the different foci of worship, will depend on local circumstances, but there needs to be thought about how the use of the candles enhances the worship and gives the right emphasis at the right moments.

Two detailed points are worth noting.

Firstly, if there are candles on the altar, then they need not be pushed to the very corners, as is often seen. The altar is a table. If one put candles on a table for supper at home, one would not arrange them on the edge. Aesthetically they look wrong there and do not help the sense of the altar as a table around which the faithful gather for a meal.

Secondly, when candles are carried in procession, again, like the cross, they are not carried to enhance the entry of the ministers. At one level their entry is purely functional; it is so that they are in place to illuminate the celebration and possibly to be carried to the lectern or the altar to highlight particular moments. At another level they are part of a procession to illuminate and honour the cross or the book of the Scriptures or whatever symbol is being brought in. The procession should be formed in such a way as to reveal that.

Mention has been made of the altar itself as a focus of the presence of Christ. For some Christians this is an odd idea, for a few it may even seem idolatrous. But for many the altar has become a focus of Christ's presence as an extension of the Eucharist itself. Because it is the place where we focus the presence of Christ in the liturgy, the altar table has itself become a sort of sacrament of Christ and his presence in the Church, and that is why it is appropriate for people to reverence it, not only in their minds, but with their bodies, bowing to it as they enter and leave the church.

It is the altar, and the altar of the celebration, to which this reverence is paid. It is not to the cross. It is not to some distant altar. Some extraordinary things happen when there is more than one altar, perhaps a 'nave altar' where the Eucharist is usually celebrated, and a 'high altar' in the distance that is not normally used for the celebration. Ministers are sometimes seen to come in, turn their backs on the altar at which the Eucharist is celebrated, and reverence this other one in the distance. No sense can be made of that.

The problem arises because there is more than one altar. In the Roman Church there would be a strong insistence on having only one altar in the main church, resiting it if necessary, but never creating a second focus. In theory this is right, for there ought to be just one table, just as there ought to be just one font, because both sacraments are about the unity of Christian people in Christ. Nevertheless a determination to remove altars can be philistine if it destroys the essential architectural design and shape of the building. Where everything about the building draws the eye to an altar at the east end, simply to remove it, or to make it the place for the president's chair, so that all points to him, is mistaken. If we are to have some sensitivity to tradition and to art, we shall sometimes have to compromise on two altars, provided they are not too close together, and provided that care is taken to make the new and central altar sufficient of a focus that the eye is not immediately drawn away from the celebration.

Where a church does opt for a second altar, it must not be of too temporary a nature. We may resist the idea of building it in stone where it is quite unmovable, and be thankful for the adaptability of modern church design where everything moves, but if the altar table moves regularly – into its central place, for instance, only when the Eucharist is to be celebrated at it – the sacrament is undervalued, and the witness of the altar to the presence of Christ undermined. The place the altar occupies for the celebration of the Eucharist should be its normal setting, even if we design it in such a way that it can, on certain occasions, be moved.

But before creating the potential confusion of a second sanctuary, and certainly in cases where the second sanctuary would be unspacious and insignificant, a church needs to consider quite seriously whether its liturgy could not be served by the use of the traditional altar at the east end, but with the major part of the Eucharist focused away from the table, in an area that included lectern and president's chair, perhaps at the chancel step. That space could be the setting, not only for everything in the service until the Greeting of Peace, but also for everything that follows the distribution.

In making these decisions, good advice is important, and there now exists a good number of examples of bad, as well as of good, practice. A church needs to bring together liturgical principles, pastoral needs and architectural realities, recognizing that all three have to be taken seriously, and the right solution found by taking all three into account. And it is not simply a matter of finding a practical solution. One has to ask: 'What does this ordering *say*?'

The president's chair

If it is true that good presidency of the Eucharist requires the priest to be visible throughout the liturgy, but not to dominate it, he needs to be able to sit down where he may be seen. If he disappears from sight his presidency begins to disintegrate. If he stands at the altar throughout, the focus remains too strongly on him. Although in the design of some new churches the need to place the president's chair, so that he may have the whole congregation within his sight, is being understood, few older churches have made this provision.

The chair itself needs to have sufficient dignity to indicate that it is the seat for the president, and to stand out from other chairs, stools and benches around it. But it is not a throne, and must not seem too grand. Quite what that means will depend on the building in which it is set. In some churches the solution has been in the use of the chair known before as 'the bishop's chair', and there is an appropriateness about that, because every president of the Eucharist is there as the bishop's representative and deputy. But, again, the danger is that the chair will be too grand.

It is important that the chair be so placed that the president can, when seated, have eye contact with the whole community, or as much of it as possible. That will sometimes mean that it cannot be in the sanctuary, but, in the design of a traditional church, will be nearer the chancel step. The fashion in some churches to use a clergy stall in the chancel, facing across the church, to preside at the first half of the Eucharist, can hardly ever serve the need. Being 'in choir' is quite a different idea from presiding at the liturgy; the angle of the chair is wrong and the desk in front is a barrier between president and people. But, as with the altar, local compromise has to be worked out. However it is done, the chair is more important than it seems. When it is in the right place and used wisely, it can transform the relationship between president and people as the liturgy is being celebrated.

Around the altar

The most important thing that needs to be around the altar is space. It is not just that, at a practical level, there needs to be room for the ministers to move around the sanctuary, though that is important. It is not even that the altar, like the lectern, needs space around it to make its impact, though that is true. It is, beyond that, that part of what people are often seeking in worship is space. Their need is for space in a different sense, a time of rest and re-creation in lives that are over-busy, in diaries that are over-cluttered, or in homes where there is no peace. But the need for that sort of space is met also through the provision of physical space. Lack of clutter and lack of fuss in the celebration of the liturgy help create it. The strongest argument for the removal from churches of the excess (often comparatively new) stalls, chairs and pews is not so much the practical one, that they are not used, or that there needs to be an area for exhibitions, coffee or whatever, but a more spiritual, as well as aesthetic, argument, that space is holy and helpful. Never more so than in the sanctuary and around the altar.

But there needs to be a credence table. There needs to be adequate provision for distributing holy communion. In some churches there needs to be also an aumbry in which to house the consecrated bread and wine to be taken to the sick and housebound.

The credence table is not a mini-altar, with candles on it. It should be inconspicuous, as far as possible out of sight, for nothing happens at it of symbolic value; it is purely functional. But if the altar is to be left uncluttered through the service and vessels placed upon it only when they are needed, the credence table needs to be of sufficient size to take all the things that ought to be there.

Adequate provision for distribution of holy communion means, chiefly, that people ought to be able to draw near to receive around the altar. There are occasions when distributing communion from a variety of different altars and stations around a building will be right, but something is lost when people do not all come in the same direction to the altar of the celebration to share around the table, and a design that makes that convergence unsatisfactory is a bad one. People are more willing now to stand to receive, but the Anglican instinct to be kneeling at this point is not to be lightly set aside (see the next chapter) and that may mean some kind of rail or bench, though every effort should be made to avoid anything that cuts the altar off from the people and places a fence around it. It should signal openness and invitation, with barriers down.

Anglican custom, since the reservation of the sacrament once again become commonplace, has been to locate the aumbry in the sanctuary, but away from the altar, and if possible in a chapel. This was in strong distinction to the Roman Catholic practice, where the

tabernacle was on the high altar. But Roman understanding is now much closer to the Anglican practice,
and insists that the reserved sacrament should not be a
focus during the celebration of the Eucharist. The
primary focus of the presence of Christ is the altar
rather than the aumbry.

There are also questions about siting and space for
musicians. These are discussed briefly in Chapter 22
and are examined very fully in the report of the
Archbishops' Commission on Church Music, *In Tune
with Heaven*.

Once these considerations relating to credence table,
distribution, aumbry and provision for musicians have
been taken into account, the primary impetus remains to
move out the clutter and preserve the space.

5

SYMBOLS AND GESTURES

The language of symbolism

One of the areas in which Anglicans have been growing together in recent years is in their use of symbolism in worship. The kind of basic questioning that Roman Catholics employed after the Second Vatican Council about their rites and ceremonies gave Anglicans in the Catholic tradition the encouragement they needed to do the same, to look at the meaning of what they were doing, to jettison practices that had either grown over-involved or else had simply lost their meaning, and to affirm the significance of a limited number of rituals that carried important Christian meaning. This simplification and this desire to use only what has appropriate meaning has enabled Anglicans of a more Evangelical tradition to re-examine their own suspicion of anything that smacked of ritual. The result is a Church in which the language of symbolism is being recovered, not least in the Eucharist.

The difficulty the Church faces is that, though there is a new openness to the power of the symbol and to the non-verbal in liturgy, it is a language that has been so long lost for many Christians that recovering it is not straightforward and easy. We do things in worship – whether it be grasping the hand of another, or lighting a candle, or raising our hands, or allowing our feet to be washed – because in the doing we express truths that defy words. In ordinary life, if we kiss somebody, or put an arm around them, the meaning, depending on the context, is clear. We do not first tell them what we are going to do, and afterwards tell them what it means. We kissed them or put our arms around them because words

54

simply would not do. The action speaks louder than words. The action has its own non-verbal language. In all sorts of settings in ordinary life we take this for granted.

We need to recover the same sense in church, but here the whole language of traditional symbolism has gone rather dead on people. In church they do things, they enact rituals. Yet not only do they not know their meaning, but it does not occur to them that there is meaning to be found. They are simply 'what we do', or, more likely, 'what we have always done'. So there is need for good and clear teaching to enable us to recover the sense of meaning, to be able to speak the language, to allow ourselves to be ministered to by sign and symbol.

But the teaching brings its own problem, for, if the symbol and the gesture express what cannot be put into words, the teaching will nearly always narrow down the meaning, always take the power out of the symbol by explaining it away. The moment I try to explain the meaning of things I do in the Eucharist, whether kneeling to confess, or bringing bread and wine to the altar, or breaking the consecrated bread, I limit the meaning to my description, yet the truth is that all these things are capable of being received at different levels, with a variety of aspects of the truth dawning on me on different occasions. Symbolism allows truth to have no end of strata, and meaning in each, and the resort to words of explanation, even to biblical warrant, can destroy that. We should be wary of explaining away what is beyond words.

Another way in which people have been able to affirm symbolism in worship rather more has been in the recovery of the sense that symbolic and ritual activity in the liturgy is not something that people watch, but something primarily in which they participate. However happy we may be to use words like 'drama' and 'theatre' about worship, it is always on the understanding that we are not spectators, audience, but part of the cast of the drama. Sometimes particular people act out something in which the size of the congregation or the church building dictate that not all can join, but they do it as representative of the whole assembled community, and through them we find ourselves caught up in it. The principal point, therefore, of any kind of ritual is not how effective it looks, but what it does to the hearts and souls of those who share in it. We draw close to God in what we do in church as well as in what we say.

Rituals under scrutiny

We need to be ready sometimes to examine the things we do and take for granted in worship, and to ask whether the meaning can still be discerned, whether that meaning is sound, and whether its message strengthens or confuses the offering of worship and the communion of the people with God. We need to be on the lookout for rituals that have lost their meaning, and for those which convey the wrong meaning, just as we also need to be looking for new rites and new symbols that communicate grace and truth with freshness.

We need to ask, for instance:

Why in some churches is the Gospel read facing north as it was in ancient Rome? In Rome is was because north was the direction in which the gospel needed to be spread, for that was where the heathen were. But are Glasgow and Edinburgh more in need of the good news than Southampton or even Marseilles?

Why in some churches do the members of the choir face east during the Gospel, turning their back on the reading from the lectern? Is it because they do not want to hear? Or is it because the Gospel used to be read from the altar and they turned towards it, but now the reading of the Gospel has moved but they haven't, because they've forgotten what they are doing and why?

Why in some churches is the high point of the liturgy the collecting and presentation of money, and its elevation at the table with great ceremony? Could it be because, when ritual is suppressed in sensitive doctrinal areas, it breaks out somewhere harmless, but then overemphasizes the action to which it attaches itself?

Why in some churches does the president say, 'We break this bread to share', and then break only sufficient for those in the sanctuary, and the people respond, 'We are one body, because we all share in one bread', and then proceed to receive their individual unbroken unshared wafers? Is it because they have always used personalized wafers, right back when they used a communion rite that didn't make much of the breaking?

Why in some churches do the people hold back when the president invites them to 'draw near', and not approach the table until all in the sanctuary have received. Is it because they believe the communion of the priest and his assistants is nothing to do with them, and that the communion of the people is something separate? Or is it just unthinking habit or natural shyness?

In all these cases, and they are only examples, parishes are either using rites and customs that have lost their meaning or acquired a poor meaning, or else are doing things they imagine have no symbolic value, but where meaning, and unfortunate meaning at that, is in reality being conveyed. Occasionally a church needs to be rigorous in examining what it does in the liturgy.

There is a need also to ensure that secondary symbolism does not obscure primary symbolism. In baptism, for instance, anointing with oil and giving candles contribute to the rite and have helpful meaning, but they become a nuisance if they obscure the primary symbol of water and the meaning its use carries.

Similarly in the Eucharist, we need to ensure that the primacy of the Scriptures and of the bread and wine are not obscured by too many other symbols and rituals, good in themselves, but capable of sowing confusion.

Body and senses

This whole area of ritual and symbol is a taking seriously of the human need to worship God not only with mind and soul, but with body and every sense. It may well be that we express our deepest worship of God when we are still and silent, and even in our pews. But even there we express our worship of God through our bodies, through the different postures we adopt, and through gestures we make with our bodies.

There is a strange suspicion of one another by those who employ different gestures, arising from different traditions of church life. Some churchpeople, who expect their clergy to raise their arms and use their hands in saying the Eucharistic Prayer, are quite incapable of coping with lay people who do exactly the same thing as they sing a song of praise. The two are doing the same thing; even the motivation is similar. Other church-people, who do raise their arms to worship, can themselves be suspicious of those who bend the knee to do so. And others, who set great store on the truth that their salvation has been won at a price upon the cross of Christ, can't quite see the point when some of their fellow Christians make the sign of that same cross on their bodies or their foreheads as they share in Christian worship.

All these people are expressing in their different ways the worship of God in the use of their bodies. The movements of the ministers in the liturgy – walking and bowing in patterns as it sometimes seems – are simply an extension of that same instinct to give God glory through the body. The movements and rhythms of those who do liturgical dance are not of another order, but a more vigorous and spontaneous interpretation of that same instinct. The movements of the liturgy are themselves a liturgical dance, and none the worse for that, provided the motivation remains giving glory to God through the body.

The body has its senses, and there is no reason why opportunity should not be given in worship for all the senses to be used in drawing close to God.

We hear, not just in the words of Scripture, but in the fine language of the liturgy, and also through the medium of music which draws so many closer to God.

We see. Although many of us were brought up to put our hands together and close our eyes to pray, we know that all around us in the liturgy is visual stimulus if we will, quite to the contrary, open our eyes wide to worship. Very often the church building itself has its own visual stimulus, whether the sheer beauty of its architecture, or what it proclaims in glass or statue, banner or poster. But, more than that, the action of the liturgy before our eyes draws us to God as we allow ourselves to look and to see.

We touch. The Eucharist invites us to touch. In some settings we may join hands to pray. We touch, whether with hesitant handclasp or affectionate embrace at the Greeting of Peace. Sometimes, within the Eucharist as in other settings, we lay on hands or receive that ministry, and there is touch there also, of a sort that puts us 'in touch' with Christ.

We taste. That is one of the great glories of eucharistic worship. Like the psalmist we 'taste and see that the Lord is good', as we receive the bread and wine over which thanks has been given.

If we are to worship God through all the senses, there is, as well as the smell of flowers, the smell of incense, though not every Anglican responds to it with delight. Its use has never been regular and widespread in the Anglican tradition since the Reformation. What seems to be happening today is that probably even fewer churches are using it at the Eucharist week by week, but more and more are using it for some special occasions.

Epiphany has always been an obvious time, with its association with the gifts of the magi, but on other great festivals too it is being used and this fifth sense employed.

At the Eucharist it can be used in one or two ways. Either it can simply be left to burn, without ceremony, providing its own special smell as a background to worship, the smoke rising up and giving some meaning to the words we use in worship 'that our prayer may come up to you as the incense'. It can burn in a pot before the altar; it does not need to be swung in a thurible. Or it may be used, in the more traditional way, to highlight moments in the service, censing the gospel book before it is read, and the altar and the bread and wine before the Eucharistic Prayer.

It is always a symbol of purification and of prayer, and 'the house filled with smoke', as in Isaiah's vision, is a reminder of the worship of heaven. It needs to be rescued from being thought 'Romish' or 'high church'. Its origins are in Scripture, and its use need not be restricted to one part of the Church. Where all the senses are to be employed, bring in the incense, but never with that kind of distracting fussiness that has often brought its use into disrepute.

Postures of prayer and praise

But the use of the body that no one can avoid is the adopting of a posture through which to worship - prostrate, seated, standing or kneeling. Which is adopted and when are usually more a matter of habit than anything else, but we need to recover more strongly an understanding of how the posture of worship helps to form attitudes to God, and how a variety of posture in the liturgy helps to express its different moods.

In the Church of England we have moved from a Prayer Book norm of kneeling for most prayer to a variety of practice that in many churches has lost the habit of kneeling altogether. I believe that the Prayer

Book's insistence on the value of kneeling, and its memorable 'meekly kneeling upon your knees' before the confession at the Eucharist, is an emphasis we discard at our peril. It is easy to see why the habit has declined so speedily, for the kind of kneeling we did was often full of discomfort. Sometimes it was half crouch, with back bent double. Often it was with backside trying to reach a pew just too far away for comfort. Occasionally it was on a high but squashy hassock. And very often it was for too long, and so simply had to be endured. Kneeling is not a suitable posture for prayer because it makes us uncomfortable. It is only suitable if it allows us to express humility, penitence and longing. It is the traditional posture to ask favours and seek forgiveness.

If we did all our praying on our knees, these aspects would gain too much prominence, and our picture of God would be warped. But, if we do no praying on our knees, but always stand as his confident children, or sit as his relaxed children, there will be another imbalance, just as detrimental to our picture of him.

In the Roman eucharistic rite, the people kneel now only for part of the Eucharistic Prayer (and that possibility is discussed in Chapter 15). If we follow our Anglican tradition we shall see kneeling as the natural posture at the Eucharist for penitence, for intercession and for communion. Except where conditions are too cramped, it would be a gain if we recovered such a practice where it has been lost, at least occasionally, perhaps in Lent.

For all that, it is a blessing that we have discovered standing as a posture for prayer, as well as for singing, and especially for prayers of praise. We can indeed thank God 'for counting us worthy to stand in [his] presence and serve'. At the Eucharist, kneeling to praise God in the *Gloria* is a pity, and to greet one another at the beginning or at the Peace a silliness, and the beginning of the Eucharistic Prayer, with its 'Lift up your hearts' ought to bring us almost on to tiptoe, even if 'Holy, holy, holy' does bring us to our knees.

As for sitting, we can value this as a posture for meditation and reflection, as well as for the attentiveness that ought to mark the Ministry of the Word. We can leave behind us the extraordinary crouch, that was neither quite kneeling nor sitting, and learn to sit straight-backed but relaxed, and find in that too another posture that opens us in a different way to God.

For those who order the liturgy and plan services there is a responsibility to see that these different postures are wisely used, that the variety is there to help express the different moods of approach, and that no one posture is retained so long that people become anxious or distressed.

The ministers and their gestures

It is difficult to prescribe the gestures that the ministers, and especially the president and the deacon at the Eucharist, should use to help draw the people into fellowship and prayer, for a gesture is such a personal thing, and every minister must discover for themselves what use of eye and arm and hand aids their communication. But it is unlikely that they will communicate well with eyes down and arms tight at their side from beginning to end, so it is something they need to foster.

It is the use of the eyes that is most crucial. Communication with eyes averted is difficult. It gives a sense of the self held back, denied to the recipients of the address. Of course there are moments when it is wrong, or at least imposes the personality of the minister when he (or she) is simply a channel, and some (not all) would feel that eye contact at the distribution of communion is a case of this. But in general we communicate more with our face, and especially with our eyes, than with our arms and hands.

But arms and hands play their part. In the days when the ministers had their backs to the people, when they extended their arms to pray, they were taught only to do so from below the elbow, in a fairly tight gesture, and that was right from the back view. When the ministers are facing the people, more expansive gestures, using the whole arm, are more effective.

Three such gestures suggest themselves. One is in normal address to the congregation, in greeting, for instance, or in invitation. It is an extending of the arms out in what is essentially an inclusive gesture towards the people. It is almost like the beginnings of an embrace. It is a relational gesture between minister and people.

A second is a gesture over the people, conveying grace, in blessing, for instance, or absolving. The minister extends his hands and arms towards and over the people, with the sense of one who is communicating to them something that is coming down from God.

The third is a gesture of prayer. Here arms and hands are raised, fingers extend upwards, in a gesture that is directed to God, and draws the eyes of the people away from the minister 'heavenwards', so to speak. The convention is for the minister to adopt this gesture when he speaks alone in prayer, for instance during the Eucharistic Prayer, but to have hands joined when everyone is praying together, but it cannot be a hard and fast rule. Yet a gesture that raises the eyes, and therefore the hearts, from the minister towards God is particularly important in these days of celebrations facing the people. If the Eucharist is to get 'off the ground', if the vertical is to come into play as well as the horizontal, something like this can help.

These are only models. There are no precise rights and wrongs in this area of worship. Ministers must find a style in which they are relaxed and in which they can feel that the people are being drawn into worship. What seems appropriate on one occasion – in a great cathedral, for instance – will suddenly feel quite inappropriate on another – perhaps in a house group Eucharist. The spontaneous gesture has its place in liturgy just as much as the spontaneous word even within a fixed form.

6

TEXTS AND TRADITIONS

The Book of Common Prayer

It is one of the paradoxes of worship in the Church of
England today that never has there been more legal
variety, and yet at some points in the year at least there
is more use of common material than for a long while.

As far as the Eucharist is concerned, there are three
orders of Holy Communion in legal use. The first is the
rite in the Book of Common Prayer of 1662. There are
those who have written it off and do not believe it has a
place today. But it is still much valued, it has a place in
the worship pattern of a very large number of churches,
and remains in any case a doctrinal standard. It ought
also to be a resource for those who want to draw older
texts into new service forms. Because this book is
principally about these newer rites, I ought to give an
account of how I see the continuation of the Prayer Book
tradition.

Some of those who value the Prayer Book rite most,
and want to use it to the exclusion of others, do so
because of its doctrinal stance. They see in all the newer
rites, at least in their mainstream form, a shift from the
Church of England's Reformation theology regarding
the Eucharist. They see also, not a confused rite in
which all sorts of liturgical principles seem to have been
turned on their head, but a highly creative and ingenious
order, with its own rationale, serving its own doctrinal
purpose. But that is probably not what attracts the
majority of those who value the Prayer Book.

For some it is its lack of variety, seasonal emphasis,
permission to insert or expand or omit, its sheer
predictability, that allows some people to pray the liturgy

at a level other than the text. It is easy to see, in this case, why what makes it attractive to some is the very thing that makes it a burden to others.

For some it is a simple thing about continuity. This is the way our ancestors worshipped. There is something marvellous about entering into their heritage, kneeling where they knelt, and saying the same words. Not everybody would think it necessary to use precisely the same rite as they to achieve that, and some might think it a rather narrow view of our Christian ancestry to limit it to those whose spirituality was shaped by the Book of Common Prayer.

Perhaps for the majority of those who hold firmly to the Prayer Book the issue is about language and literature. It is not just a cultural argument that those who grow up unused to the King James Bible and the Prayer Book are missing something as crucial as Shakespeare in terms of English culture and identity. It is that the language of modern liturgy can be terse, lacking poetry and rhythm, and is sometimes banal. It is about this issue of language that this chapter will be mainly concerned.

No one will be drawn entirely by one argument, and all these may be present in attitudes people hold; but it is useful to see what contributes to their sense of unease at the neglect of the Prayer Book in the Church today.

Those who have no time for the Prayer Book suspect other motives of its defenders or think them simply out of touch with the reality of life in modern Britain. Perhaps people like the Prayer Book because it doesn't disturb them. Perhaps it is part of a nostalgia among those who do not want to face life as it really is today. And isn't this talk about culture, Shakespeare and poetry coming out of a very narrow educational and social sector of society? It is all worlds away from 'Neighbours' and 'Coronation Street'.

It has become a stale sort of argument, with very little listening going on. I believe that there is a future for the Prayer Book tradition. I rather regret that the Prayer

Book Communion rite is untouchable in terms of loosening up and modification, because I believe it could be made much more usable without losing any of its essential qualities. But any such suggestion is, perhaps not surprisingly, misunderstood and met with suspicion, even though what Prayer Book people very often love is not the Book of Common Prayer, but its proposed revision of 1928. I do not believe that, as it stands, the Prayer Book will very often meet the needs of the Church on great occasions when a rich diversity of people come together to celebrate, though I do believe that material from it might find a place within such celebrations. I do believe that it has found its natural place in the Church of today as the rite of the quiet celebration. I do not think that is pushing it to the edge of church life, because we need to encourage the quiet celebration as much as the Family Eucharist approach with all its variety and vigour. I cannot see that its use in every church community can be justified today. But I do believe that it is a tradition that needs to be affirmed, and that a Church of England without it, and without it *in use*, would be a Church cutting itself off from its roots, and both liturgically and spiritually impoverished.

Rites and freedoms

Alongside the Prayer Book rite stand the two orders of Holy Communion in The Alternative Service Book. Rite A is the normative modern language rite of the Church, and was the fruit of liturgical revision through the 1960s and 1970s that concentrated on the Eucharist much more than any other service form. It differs from the Prayer Book in language, in theological emphasis, in structure, and in the freedoms it permits. It has established itself very widely in the Church, and few expect to see its basic style, shape or structure abandoned at the end of the century, when its present authorization runs out. There is pressure to tighten up some loose ends, to provide better texts at certain points and to extend the permission to substitute other authorized or suitable words at points where variety is not now permitted. But no radical change is contemplated.

Rite B is, to some people's thinking, neither flesh nor fowl. Depending somewhat on the options employed, it moves between Prayer Book language and an almost contemporary style, and between the theological emphases of the Reformation and a more contemporary understanding. Its variety is more in the choice between these two strands, than a more general permission to enrich by the inclusion of other texts, but the structure is similar to that of Rite A. If the Prayer Book rite could be loosened up a little, and Rite A users encouraged more to draw on traditional texts, Rite B would lose its rationale. Meanwhile it serves a purpose and is a kind of bridge between old and new.

The possibilities for enrichment of the Eucharist at various points by drawing in other texts, not all of them new, have been extended by the publication, with varying degrees of synodical and episcopal commendation, of three further service books. *Lent, Holy Week, Easter* (1986) and *The Promise of His Glory* (1991) provide for the Easter and Christmas cycles (see Chapter 7), but much of their material is a useful resource outside the seasons for which they were originally written. *Patterns for Worship* (1989) goes further and, if its recommendations receive approval, will push back some of the boundaries of freedom and variety. Most of its material is available for legal use, simply because it provides, like many other books of prayers that have no official status, material at points where (in Holy Communion Rite A) variety is permitted. Other parts go beyond that and would have to face the rigorous process of synodical revision. They would allow, among other things, authorized alternatives in Rite A to the Creed and the present Penitential Prayers and Eucharistic Prayers. They would allow also, on occasions, for a more radical loosening up of the rite (and the implications of this are discussed in Chapter 19).

Common prayer and the limits of diversity

It may be that *Patterns for Worship* will prove to be the furthest that the Church of England will go in permitting diversity, for although *Patterns for Worship* tries to insist on what the Church needs to have in common in its liturgy, it also permits variations beyond what has been allowed before. It would be wrong to see recent books as intended to undermine common prayer. *Patterns for Worship* sets out to bring back into the fold, so to speak, those who have wandered much further down the path to congregational worship. It seeks to show why the Church must set constraints in some areas, as well as signalling some areas where less constraint is needed. *Lent, Holy Week, Easter* and *The Promise of His Glory* provide rites for the major Christian festivals that will encourage their celebration in a common form throughout the Church.

Nevertheless, the mood of the Church is to recover, at some points at least, that sense of common prayer that the proliferation of liturgies has dissipated. This is not the same issue as a return to the Prayer Book. Common Prayer is not the prerogative of those who most value that book. Common Prayer is simply prayer that the whole Church shares, be it very traditional or very modern.

Anglican identity is very much tied up with this concept of common prayer. For Anglicans have traditionally pointed to their liturgy as the source both of their doctrine and of their unity. The Book of Common Prayer has always been regarded as a doctrinal standard, more obviously so than the 39 Articles of Religion. If Anglican doctrine is to be found in its liturgy, but then each congregation sets its own service forms, where is the objective doctrine of the Church to be found? If Anglicans look to liturgy to find their unity, to reveal their 'family relationship' across the world, where is that unity to be found if, not only every province, but every parish within the province, does its own thing? Nothing less than the identity and integrity of Anglicanism is at stake.

For that reason, as well as for the more practical and pastoral reason that people visiting different churches around the country want to feel at home in the worship they encounter wherever they go, the Church has to stand out for common prayer, and to set limits to legitimate diversity. In our multicultural situation, and with a strong impetus to an evangelism that will take the gospel into new settings, those constraints must not be too tight.

We cannot, for instance, sensibly return to a single eucharistic liturgy with a single eucharistic prayer. On the other hand, if *Patterns for Worship* is authorized in something like its present form and, additionally, the synod provides eucharistic prayers for use with children as it has set its mind to do, the Church of England will have no less than fourteen eucharistic prayers. Perhaps that can be permitted through a short period of upheaval, but if we emerge into the next century with that sort of variety, and the *laissez-faire* attitude that prevails towards those who press the boundaries even further by using unauthorized material, either from another Church or of their own devising, in what sense is there common prayer at one of the most significant moments in the Eucharist?

Patterns for Worship sees common prayer preserved by careful and satisfying base structures and some familiar 'core' texts. The debate of course is about how much 'core' there should be. People would accept more of the liturgy as 'core' - normative texts for such regular use that they become memorized - if the texts were of sufficient quality to satisfy the soul.

It is probably fanciful to hope that there might be agreement in the Church about a translation of the Bible for use in the liturgy. The ASB provides its samples of four, but all of them predate the Revised English Bible, the New International Version, The New Jerusalem Bible and the New Revised Standard Version that compete for the market today. There have been tremendous gains from this industry of Bible translation; the Scriptures have come alive again in the Church in a wonderful way. But the price that has been paid is the disappearance of the common familiar text, parts of which people committed to memory, and whole phrases that become part of everyone's speech. However many translations we use and compare in study, in liturgy we need to be fed by words that by their familiarity become lodged deep within us.

The Church ought at least to try to find a way forward that will allow this to be. At the very least, each individual congregation should decide which translation it will almost invariably use, and stay with it; but this is very much second best to common Scripture throughout the Church.

Treasures old and new

One of the lessons we can learn from the last few years of liturgical change is that in worship old and new can exist fruitfully side by side. Perhaps it was right, as well as inevitable, that in the 1960s and 1970s those who worked on the reform of the eucharistic liturgy believed that there needed to be a consistency of literary style. Archaic language could have no place in a modern rite, and so, apart from a rubric to permit historic texts when sung and another to allow the Lord's Prayer in its traditional version, ASB Rite A proceeded on the assumption that there needed to be a new liturgical language, and no ancient texts came through unscathed.

There were three categories of text. There were those that were newly composed, fresh creations. Inevitably they were uneven in quality, but the better among them have proved the most popular texts of the new rite. People particularly responded to the work of David Frost, not least in the Prayer after Communion, 'Father of all, we give you thanks and praise . . .'.

Secondly there were old Prayer Book texts modernized. These have not been so popular, partly because the little alterations made people stumble; and some changes seemed petty and obscure. But at least these were English texts revised in England.

The third category, and the one that has won least acceptance, has been the set of texts that have been revised internationally through ICET (The International Consultation on English Texts). Here the basic text from which work began has not been an English one, but a Latin one, and the translations often owe nothing to the language of the English Prayer Book of 1662. The motive, of course, was excellent and the scholarship first-rate. It seemed the right way forward to have international and ecumenical texts for the whole English-speaking Christian world – a new and wider 'common prayer'.

A generation on, we find ourselves wondering whether everything needed to be updated. New texts of course should be written in a thoroughly contemporary style, not in a phoney imitation of the sixteenth or seventeenth century. But Prayer Book material perhaps could have been left as it was, or at least as a permissible alternative to a stab at a new version. And the new version would probably be better when it was a new prayer, rather than a tinkering with the old. And, as for international and ecumenical texts, for all the attractiveness of that as an idea, does it sufficiently root a liturgy in its own culture? Is it wrong to want words that are distinctively English or Anglican?

To be fair to the liturgists, it was not always they who led the Church down the path it took. In relation, for instance, to that text in the Eucharist usually called 'The Prayer of Humble Access', the Liturgical Commission did not want to alter Cranmer's text, 'We do not presume . . .', and wrote instead a new prayer,

> Most merciful Lord,
> your love compels us to come in.
> Our hands were unclean,
> our hearts were unprepared . . .

that picks up the feel and resonance of Cranmer's original, but is not confused with it and has a contemporary ring. It was the General Synod that would not have it and insisted instead on tinkered Cranmer. But there is a new mood now to retain and enjoy the best of the old and at the same time to create the new, and to mix the two together in liturgy, just as we have always in any one service sung hymns from different centuries and cultures and been enriched by the variety.

This is part of the hope for the Prayer Book tradition. Alongside the use of the Prayer Book rite much as it stands, where that is appropriate, we may hope for the imaginative use in new rites of some of the fine texts we have inherited, including of course the ones that we are used to singing and hearing sung. Why not, for instance, the Prayer Book's fine confessions (from Morning Prayer and from the Communion rite) at the Rite A Eucharist on the Sundays of Lent?

But, alongside this, there must be the sensitive creation of new texts. The folly of Anglicanism through many decades was, not that it stayed with its Prayer Book, but that it did not add in every age to its splendours. Today there must be fresh writing, emerging from our own situation without being the slave of every theological fashion. We need to work away, and be prepared to use and to discard, until we have rediscovered a liturgical style that combines deeply satisfying cadences with clarity of communication. And it would be good if the Church's 'wordsmiths' were given encouragement as they develop this, rather than the carping criticism they have too often received. The search for a new liturgical language is not easy, but it has to be pursued, for a return only to old forms spells death. Wise householders produce from their store both the old and the new.

Celebrating the feminine

One of the concerns of those who work on new texts must be to affirm and enhance the feminine in our

Christian tradition. The Church has moved more slowly in England than in other parts of the English-speaking world to respond to the demand for changes in language that make more explicit the inclusion and value of the feminine. This is a difficult area, about which some people (not all of them women) feel very strongly, and which others see as no issue at all, a piece of fashionable silliness that will pass away. It is not a controversy that this book can examine, but nor is it quite irrelevant to it.

The feminine is affirmed in the Eucharist, not only by texts, but by the manner of the celebration and the part women play in it (see also in Chapter 2). Nevertheless it is in the words that we say that we give important signals about what we believe. Maybe it is true, as many would say, that when we say, 'live in love and peace with all men', 'against you and against our fellow men' and 'his perfect sacrifice made once for the sins of all men', we are including women, but the plain fact is that some of them are not feeling included, and quite certainly the feminine is not being much affirmed, let alone celebrated.

Not everyone will believe that this problem should be met by altering texts, though the three examples above can all be amended with no loss of rhythm or meaning. But at very least there ought to be a sensitivity about this issue in those who lead worship, and a recognition that new texts should seek to redress an imbalance in the tradition. It is possible to do this, and to do it in an exciting way, without compromising the Church's belief about either God or our human nature.

In this book attention is drawn to some of the slight modifications in Rite A that the Liturgical Commission's *Making Women Visible* suggests, to begin to meet this sensitivity, one that some would call an injustice too.

The meaning of words

In thinking about the words of worship, I make a plea that we take seriously the meaning of the words we use. We need to do this not only at the level of believing the words of faith we proclaim and praying from the heart the prayers we say with our lips. At a much simpler and practical level we want liturgical words to mean what they say. When we say, 'We break this bread', bread needs to be broken, not left unbroken on the plate. When we say, 'Draw near with faith', we want to see people get up and come. When we say, 'Go in peace', we want them to go, not settle down for the notices or sing another hymn. So often in liturgy we use words as if they are pleasing ritual noises that somehow don't carry the literal meaning they would in any other context.

Some might say it doesn't matter. No great harm is done if people, once invited to go in peace, are nevertheless kept back to sing a hymn. But harm *is* done if that sort of use of language fosters in people a sense that what is said in church is somehow not real. How are they to distinguish between the words we apparently don't take seriously, for they are just pleasing sounds, and the ones we do take seriously, and probably expect them to take seriously? Why should baptismal promises or marriage vows not be much the same thing – a pleasing sound but somehow not real? We owe it to people, if we want them to take the words of worship seriously, to mean what we say. We ask no less of them.

7

MOODS AND CYCLES

The Church's Year

One of the joys of liturgy in the Church of England in recent years has been the rediscovery of the variety of the Christian year and an increasingly rich provision for its celebration. Here the Book of Common Prayer is at its weakest. In the Eucharist, beyond the Collect, Epistle and Gospel, only the Proper Preface to the *Sanctus*, on eight Sundays or principal Holy Days of the year, introduces a seasonal flavour, though of course generations of church people have supplemented this with hymnody, and choirs with anthems, that give each day and season its distinctive feel.

In the past one of the odd effects of this invariability in the liturgy was that the need for seasonal services was met through non-eucharistic special forms. The high point of Christmas might well have been the Festival of Nine Lessons and Carols, based on Archbishop Benson's model created for Truro and popularized by King's College, Cambridge. Good Friday came to be marked more by a three–hour preaching service, that originated with the Jesuits in South America, or by Stainer's *Crucifixion*, than by the liturgy in which by eating and drinking the faithful might proclaim Christ's death till he comes.

We may be glad that the Church of England has developed a skill for fine liturgy that is not always eucharistic. There does not need to be Holy Communion with everything. But it is a pity when the Eucharist itself does not celebrate as finely as anything the great Christian mysteries of the Church's year. The new provision for seasonal material that the ASB allowed was therefore much welcomed, and this has been built upon since by *Lent, Holy Week, Easter, The Promise of His Glory*, and, most recently, to complete the provision for the whole annual cycle, by the work of some members of the Liturgical Commission in *Enriching the Christian Year* (SPCK 1993). These three books provide forms, not only for the distinctive and special rites of particular days – the procession with candles at Candlemas, the washing of feet on Maundy Thursday, the Easter Liturgy, for instance – but for seasonal texts at a whole series of points through the ordinary celebration of the Eucharist on each festival and in every season of the year. Thus, within these three books, we find seasonal provision, beyond the sentences, collect and readings, for

> The Prayers of Penitence
> Canticles for the Ministry of the Word
> The Greeting of Peace
> The Eucharistic Preface
> The Breaking of Bread
> The Invitation to Communion
> The Prayer after Communion
> The Blessing.

Here is a rich resource for the Eucharist. But a *resource* is precisely what it is. If good liturgy is a blend of the familiar and the special, there will be very few occasions when all the possible variable material should be employed. Worship is not helped by too many new words with their fresh ideas pouring out one after the other. There is also a danger of being over-seasonal and over-thematic (see below), so that season or theme becomes the master, rather than the servant, of the worship. The minister must learn to be selective.

Some of the major holy days of the year have their own special rites. There is something distinctive to insert into the worship. Insertion is exactly what does need to happen. People are helped more by finding an insertion into their regular worship than by the whole rite being turned on its head. Rarely should a special rite replace the beginning of the Eucharist, for it is in that familiar pattern of prayer, perhaps penitence, and Scripture that people settle into the rhythm of worship in which they will become open to what is to follow.

So it is that the *normal* place for the insertion of a special rite is between the Ministry of the Word and the Peace. This, of course, is how it works when Baptism or Marriage or the Laying on of hands for Healing is celebrated within the Eucharist. But it is the same place adopted for the Liturgy of Penitence on Ash Wednesday, for the Foot Washing on Maundy Thursday, for the Liturgy of the Cross on Good Friday. Where, locally, a special rite or ceremony is to be inserted this will often be the right place. Whatever is special is then caught up in the continuing movement of the liturgy in the Eucharistic Prayer and the sharing of communion. Care needs to be taken however to see that Prayers of Intercession do not too often fall victim to special insertions at this point.

The time between the Ministry of the Word and the Peace may be the normal place. But of course there are rites that demand a different shape. Palm Sunday has its own pre-rite outside. Candlemas, Maundy Thursday and All Souls all make special provision after communion. But, again, the basic shape of the Eucharist still stands out, much familiar material is still employed, and people are not therefore deprived of the rhythms of their worship.

Liturgy and the rhythms of life

But why is the Christian year important? It will of course always mean more to some than others. Even back in New Testament times Paul found that some people valued holy days, and others thought each day much the same as another. But, if we take the liturgical cycle seriously, I think we shall discover that it is of value to many more than treasure it now.

It is not exactly a historical exercise, a reconstruction of the great events in the life of Jesus and the early

Church in order that we may be well taught about them, or even that we may be thankful about them, though that does not come amiss. It is by entering into the moods and rhythms of the Christian year, and thus of Jesus in his birth and death and resurrection, that we let him into the moods and rhythms of our life, and find him helping us to live through them in faith, to be tested by them but not destroyed by them, to grow close to God through them. His life and our lives interact in the living of the Christian year. His response to his experiences shapes our own as we celebrate the Christian year. If we go deep enough, in its moods and rhythms Christ shows us how to live and also how to die.

That is a difficult truth to express. People can begin to see it as they keep Holy Week, but less obviously it applies also to the whole Christian cycle. In a way of course one can only make sense of it across a lifetime, for the whole point of a cycle is that it has no beginning and no end, but keeps going round.

For this reason it is important not to destroy the cycle by too many intrusions into it. Especially from Advent to Epiphany, and from Lent to the day of Pentecost, the Christian year has its own shape and logic and subtlety, and other special observances, local themes, anniversaries and even the intrusion of saints' days can cut across it, sometimes creatively, but more often destructively, so that the rhythm and the mood are lost.

It is important also to be wary of marking special days by a new experiment every year. Christian worship is enriched by the innovative (though very little we devise is actually new; we rediscover more than we create). If people were not encouraged to try new things, to modify tradition imaginatively, and to adapt to the circumstances of their day and their community, worship would wither. Yet some of the rites the Church has given us make their mark upon us because they keep coming back. They become part of the rhythm of our lives, and each time we encounter them we go a little deeper. Whether it be ash on our forehead at the Eucharist on

Ash Wednesday, or a candle lit for our departed at the
Eucharist on All Souls' Day, it needs to become part of
us. We must therefore be able to depend upon it. It will
happen each year; it will not too often give way to
somebody's good new idea.

Theme and flavour

One of the changes that the ASB brought to the Eucharist
was a highly thematic approach. The intention was
never that it should be oppressively so, and thus the
Sunday themes are hidden away near the back of the
book. But the lectionary relates the readings very closely
to one another (and introduces some obscure ones to
achieve it) and the collects often reflect the same theme
quite strongly. Books of recommended hymns and songs,
and even weekly outlines for intercession, followed from
various publishers, giving more and more emphasis to
the weekly theme.

At first this was widely welcomed. The Eucharist was
given a new unity by the definite theme that ran through
it, and certainly the thematic service can be ideal for
teaching purposes. But there has been a reaction against
the highly thematic approach. There has been a recognition that a general 'flavour' that comes with a season
provides a contrast with other days and seasons that is
helpful, but that a very specific theme narrows down the
liturgy. In any case some of the ASB themes seem a bit
thin, especially the twelfth time round, and in a few
cases a little too representative of the 1970s out of which
they sprang. But that is not the heart of the problem.
More important is the need to keep the Eucharist broad.
People are coming to it week by week with so many
different needs, hopes, gratitudes and sorrows, and they
need to find in the worship, whatever the season, and
whatever the contents of the readings and the sermon,
space to express what is in their hearts. Theme there
may be, but it does not need to take over every stage of
the rite to the exclusion of all others. Like any good

drama, the Eucharist can sustain a host of sub-plots as well as its central theme. That theme, in any case, is always more about the death and resurrection of Christ than about 'The Witnessing Community' or 'Those in Authority'.

In the long term there is likelihood of a new lectionary, and already the beginnings of it in *Lent, Holy Week, Easter* and *The Promise of His Glory*, as well as less thematic collects. Meanwhile what the ASB provides is adequate, provided that it is used with a sensitivity to flavour, but sitting light to theme.

Contrasting moods

One of the keys to giving to the stages of the Christian year their distinctive character is the ability to create contrast between one season and another. The seasonal material in the books already mentioned is part of this, but there is much more besides.

There is the opportunity to change the mood of the Eucharist by what is omitted and what is added. In a season like Advent or Lent, the omission of, for instance, the *Gloria*, and the provision of a fuller penitential section will contrast with the season that has gone before. Use of the Eucharistic Prayers, not on the basis of running through the sequence each four weeks, but on the basis of one for a season – in Rite A, Prayer 1 for Easter, 2 for Advent, 3 for Christmas and 4 for Lent – is an obvious starting point. Easter, of course, has its distinctive greeting and dismissal, and cascades of Alleluias at every opportunity.

Contrast can also be expressed through posture. Easter used to be distinctive because nobody *knelt* to pray. Perhaps, in churches where people normally stand for penitence and for the Eucharistic Prayer, Advent and Lent might be marked out by kneeling for these parts. On the other hand, a community that kneels for intercession might choose to stand to do so from Easter

Day to Pentecost. The change of posture introduces a change of mood.

The use of flowers, plants and foliage, and also the changing liturgical colours (see the next chapter) all make their contribution.

But much of this is undermined if the choice of music – hymns and songs, anthems and voluntaries – cuts insensitively across it. The mood and the contrast with other times has to be a matter of liaison between clergy and musicians.

All these contribute to the mood of the season. They do not make their impact in one day. But if they become the hallmarks of the season, through four, five or six weeks, they help create the rhythm of the year.

As far as special festival days, rather than whole seasons, are concerned, contrast of mood can also be a matter of time of day. The tendency to move all the major festivals to the nearest Sunday (*The Promise of His Glory* encourages this, for instance, for All Saints' Day and Candlemas) has the advantage of ensuring the attendance of more of the church community than on a weekday. The loss, however, comes in the fact that every festival acquires a kind of sameness when celebrated in the Sunday mid-morning slot. Christmas is appropriately a feast of the middle of the night; people are sensitive to that. But other festivals have their natural time: Easter at dawn, Good Friday in the afternoon, Ascension at midday, and some that are at their best in darkness, like All Saints' and Candlemas, in the evening. Most parishes have lost the tradition of the very early Communion. There are times when that, as much as the evening Eucharist, might help to give particular days their own distinctive character in the cycle of the Christian year.

8

CLOTHING AND COLOURS

Why vestments?

Canon law does not permit the minister at public worship to dispense with the customary robes and vestments. That has not prevented a number abandoning them in favour of the everyday, or in some cases the Sunday, clothes of modern life. It is difficult to make out a case against this on every occasion, but perhaps the case for distinctive liturgical clothing needs restating.

There is another side. I know five arguments in favour of vestments of some kind or other, at least for the president of the Eucharist.

The first is about origins, history and continuity. I am doubtful about the view that vestments are a natural development from the everyday clothes of Jesus and his disciples, though I have heard that taught. There is more of a case for seeing their origin in the ordinary dress of the Roman gentleman at the time when the Church emerged from persecution. But their significance lies more in their historical continuity in Western Christendom than in their precise origins. Priests and deacons at the altar for the Eucharist have worn these vestments through fifteen hundred years. They have modified them; they have been preserved from fashion no more than other clothes. But the continuity has been there, and their use today is one way of rooting what we do in the Eucharist with what the Church has always done.

That argument is, of course, the precise reason why some have wanted to abandon the use of the traditional eucharistic vestments of Western Christianity. They would want to say that what the Church did at the

Reformation was to make a break with medieval doctrine, and the vestments were part of the way that doctrine was expressed. They have feared that a return to these vestments in the Church of England marks a return to unacceptable doctrine. To reassure them, canon law affirms that they have no doctrinal significance.

A second reason for their use is that those in the sanctuary are engaged in a great drama, and for this they need, not the practical clothes of daily life, but the long flowing garments of the liturgy, garments that are pleasing to the eye and are suited to the spaciousness of the liturgy and its movements. The argument has its weak point in the fact that everybody, the whole congregation, is a participant in the drama, and logic might suggest that everyone, on entering the church, should put on a white robe. Nevertheless, if we accept that certain people have a representative function in worship, and also that in the use of our senses in worship the visual is important, the case is well-made. Where a group of people share in liturgical dance, there is nearly always a degree of uniform to what they wear; it may be the black leotard, rather than the white alb, but there is a recognition that the clothing needs to suit the task.

There is also a recognition that excessive individualism destroys the unity or distracts from what is important. Though we must be ourselves as we lead worship (see Chapter 3), there is a proper restraint in the use of our own personalities, and personality is very often expressed through clothes. There is nothing false or wrongly theatrical about dressing for a role.

The vestments of the ministers also prevent them from being classified in a way that makes them belong to only part of the congregation. If I lead worship in a three-piece suit I send out one set of signals about where I belong socially. If I wear jeans and sweat-shirt I send out different signals. In a strange way there is something neutral about vestments that do not make me the property of any particular group.

The final argument is about focus and justifies the colourful and often striking vestments of president and deacon. In the liturgy the eye needs to be drawn to where the action is, whether at lectern, altar or chair. If all the colour in the church is static, whether in the windows or on the walls or on the altar, the eye is not drawn to the liturgy itself as it moves around the building. What the ministers wear should make sufficient impact to focus the eyes on the celebration, but not so much impact as to detract from it.

The vesture of the ministers

Although some regret the gradual disappearance of the long and full English surplice as part of the vesture of the minister at the Eucharist, whether worn with the stole, or, less commonly, with the black scarf, the alb has established itself, right across the traditions of the Church, as a convenient and seemly basic garment for the leadership of worship. To it the president adds the stole and, in some places, the chasuble. Changes in styles of stoles and chasubles are partly a response to the circumstances of the new liturgy, where the president is facing the people over the altar, and where more expansive gestures become appropriate. But vestments must suit a building, as much as a liturgy, and the style of the building, the quality of light, the basic stone colours, as much as any colour within the building in glass or carpet, for instance, needs to influence the choice. Some of the modern styles, with strong primary colours, are designed to draw the eye to the celebration in new buildings where walls are often plain and glass uncoloured. Something very different and much more subtle is needed in an ancient building already full of colour. A parish often needs the help of someone with an expert eye for this. Buying by catalogue will hardly ever do.

Whether the president wears a chasuble will be partly a matter of his and the Church's theological tradition,

but it can also be influenced by the style of the
celebration and the number of robed ministers involved.
Where the priest stands alone, or almost so, at the altar,
it does not need an expansive and colourful garment to
indicate his presidency of the rite. In a sanctuary with
many ministers, lay and ordained, in their white albs, it
does need this. Setting and style of celebration ought to
influence policy and practice in these things.

Not that in this area the minister is free to decide
without consultation. Because this has been a sensitive
doctrinal issue in the past, the question of dress for the
priest at the Eucharist is protected by canon law. Any
change in a church's custom needs to be by resolution of
the Parochial Church Council. The minister, including
any visiting minister (even the bishop) has no right to
substitute his or her own preference for the locally
established custom.

The distinctive sign of the deacon at the Eucharist is
the stole worn over the left shoulder and, instead of the
chasuble, the dalmatic. In the current Roman practice, a
priest never wears his stole deacon-style, even if fulfilling
some of the deacon's traditional ministry. But this is
because, in the Roman way of seeing things, he will
nearly always be a 'concelebrant', exercising his priestly
ministry. In Anglican terms, the logic is that, when a
priest is exercising his ministry as a deacon, when he is
the deacon of the Eucharist, he dresses for that role,
with the stole as the deacon wears it. As for the dalmatic,
like the chasuble for the president, it marks the deacon
out, among a variety of ministers, and it indicates
something about the shared leadership of the Eucharist
that president and deacon have if their vestments are
complementary.

Should servers and those who assist with the
distribution of communion be specially robed? It can be
argued both ways. These are essentially ministries 'out
of the congregation' by people who otherwise sit in
among the people. That is made the clearer if, when they
take their turn at the altar, it is in their ordinary clothes.

And yet, if their role involves a visual part in an unfolding drama, they may need, just as much as the ordained ministers, to wear garments appropriate to that drama. That may argue for a different answer on Sundays and weekdays, and a different answer between those in the sanctuary throughout the celebration, and those who come up to do one thing and then return. So much depends on the building, the style of the worship, and local custom. It is not an area where great principles are at stake.

The liturgical colours

Liturgical colours for the Eucharist, both for the vestments of the ministers and the hangings of the altar and the sanctuary, need not be as uniform as they seem to have become. In England there have been the alternative sequences of Rome and Sarum, though these only emerged in their present precise form in the nineteenth century. Most churches have opted for the Roman. But, in the end, there are few rights and wrongs, and the provision of different colours for different days is about variety and even more about contrast. You come into church on Advent Sunday or Easter Day or Pentecost, and the colour has changed, signalling a change of mood.

A church might simply have three colours, festal (best), ordinary, and plain (penitential). The festal might not be white, and the plain might not be purple, but providing there was a local customary use, those who worshipped regularly would soon learn to read the signals and enjoy the contrasts. Where a church has not three colours, but six or seven, the sequence will be more complicated, but the principle the same.

That said, it may be useful to give the rationale of the Roman four-colour sequence in general use in the Church of England.

White (or gold) is for the festival seasons, Christmas to Candlemas (or sometimes Epiphany), and Easter to Pentecost Eve, on the feast days of Christ and of the Blessed Virgin Mary, and on the days of saints who were not martyrs, or on days that commemorate something other than their martyrdom. It is the festal ('best') colour, and so is used for any sort of festival, except where red has a special claim, for the Dedication Festival, for All Saints' Day, for Maundy Thursday, at weddings, often for Baptism, sometimes at a funeral.

Red has two sorts of use. Red for blood and red for a king both make it the colour of Holy Week (except Maundy Thursday). It also makes it the obvious colour for the Sundays of the Kingdom that *The Promise of His Glory* introduces in November between All Saints' Day and Advent. Red for blood also makes it the colour for the martyrs, and, since all the apostles and evangelists except John are venerated as martyrs, for their festivals too.

But red is also for tongues of flame at Pentecost, and so for the Holy Spirit. Red is therefore the colour for the last day of Easter, the Day of Pentecost, and for any other occasion that celebrates the gift of the Spirit. As such it is used increasingly for ordinations, and there is a good case for its use in Baptism, instead of the more usual white.

Purple (or blue in the Sarum tradition) is for penitence, prayer and preparation, and so is used for Advent and for Lent up till Palm Sunday (though some churches have a sackcloth 'Lenten array'). It is the normal colour for funerals, expressing the penitence and prayer very proper to the occasion. Some, of course, would prefer white to express the resurrection hope. Where this is the custom there needs to be consistency; white for some and purple for others suggests a judgement we cannot make.

Green is the colour of growth and belongs to the remaining days of the year, the ordinary days, between

Candlemas (or sometimes Epiphany) and Lent, and from the day after Pentecost Sunday until All Saints' Eve.

As for those other days that every community has, with their special themes and emphases, local decisions need to be made, consistent with the sequence of colours normally used and designed to achieve contrast and signal change, when that is the aim.

Precise rules in this area do not matter much. But one thing does. Lovely vestments, fine fabrics and a variety of colours all witness to the truth that we do not leave in the natural world outside the church the glories of creation, but delight ourselves and honour the creator by employing them in his worship. They are all his gift and they give him glory.

Part III

PREFATORY NOTE

In the ten chapters of Part III the celebration of the Eucharist is examined stage by stage. The rite used is Holy Communion Rite A of the Alternative Service Book and the section numbers refer to those in that rite. But much of the material applies also to Rite B and to the rites of other churches and provinces, and some of it also to the Communion Service of the Book of Common Prayer.

These chapters assume a norm of a Sunday Eucharist with singing. Adjustments and omissions need to be made when applying the material to other settings for the Eucharist. The majority does, nevertheless, still apply.

9

COMING IN

Preparation

Few people arrive at church for the Eucharist ready and prepared. Among families, for instance, there has been the squabbling over the bathroom, the disagreement over what clothes should be worn, and the argument about who sits where in the car. Or it may be that the phone has rung just as you were on your way. People do not always walk through the church door on the tiptoe of expectation, bursting with praise, and wholly open for the Spirit to pour in. Nor do they arrive feeling like a congregation, an assembly. They arrive as individuals, their own needs to the fore, and very often find themselves being asked to share with people they have not seen in the intervening six days since the last Sunday morning.

Only on the very special days of the Christian year do any but the most liturgically aware come with a clear view of what today's celebration will bring. What will be its flavour and its mood? How will it be different from the other Sundays?

Rite A calls the first part of the service 'The Preparation'. It is a recognition that we need to be got ready when we come in. We need to be got ready for communication with God. We also need binding together with our neighbours if we are genuinely to be a congregation and the Body of Christ. We need to begin to understand what it is that we are specially to celebrate or reflect on in this day's Eucharist. We need preparing. That is the function of this first part of the rite.

In some churches today people prepare for worship by the singing of songs and choruses for ten minutes or so before 'the service proper' begins. It is a recognition of the same thing that liturgy has nearly always seen, that we need time to warm up – to God, to each other and to what we are to celebrate. Everything between the greeting and the Collect is warming up material, serving the same need as the less liturgical chorus or song.

Entry

In some communities, the moments before the liturgy begins seems the best time to give out any notices, especially if they are to relate to the service itself. What makes little sense is for the president to do this, in advance of a more formal entry and his greeting to the people. Notices, if they are given now, need delegating to the deacon or to another minister or lay officer.

The entry of the ministers through the congregation and their approach to the altar, probably during the opening singing, has a liturgical significance. It should be designed so that the procession moves among the people, and is not simply an entry from right or left somewhere in front of them. In moving through the congregation the ministers in a sense gather its members up together and symbolically take them on towards the sanctuary. The symbolism is also present that the ministers, clergy and laity alike, are drawn out of the congregation. In a sense that is where they begun. There is the further idea of pilgrimage. On special occasions the whole people may move together towards the altar of God; but at least week by week in the movement of the ministers there is a sense of approach, moving on and drawing near. All this meaning is there as the procession moves through the church. But it needs to be ordered sensitively, so that it does convey that meaning, rather than the ministers going to their special place leaving everyone else behind.

It is probably best if this procession does not include the choir, even when it is robed. They are better in place before ever any singing begins, and in any case their progress to their seats does not carry the same meaning as the procession of the president and other ministers to the sanctuary.

The cross may be part of the procession, but, as has been said already (see Chapter 4) the emphasis is on the cross being brought in by the ministers rather than on the cross leading the ministers in.

A book may also be brought in. This is either the Bible, or a lectionary with all the readings for the day, or a Book of the Gospels, sometimes itself seen as an icon 'of Christ. By tradition the deacon, who will read the Gospel, carries it in, holding it high, and places it either on the lectern, or, if it is to be used only for the Gospel and to form part of a gospel procession, on the altar. This bringing in of the book, which is common to both Roman Catholic and Presbyterian worship, parallels the bringing in of the bread and wine as the service moves from word to sacrament, and indicates something about the equal value we accord to them.

Gathering Song

Rite A begins: 'At the entry of the ministers AN APPROPRIATE SENTENCE may be used; and A HYMN, A CANTICLE, or A PSALM may be sung.'

Because what we sing in church has undergone such a revolution in recent years, at least in some church communities, there is danger of confusion whenever instructions like this appear. In some places a distinction is drawn between 'hymn' and 'song'. As for a 'canticle', the word simply means 'song', even if we sometimes use it to describe only songs, other than psalms, that are in the Bible. Sufficient to say here that, wherever the word 'hymn' is used, there is no narrow definition. It means, 'Jesus stand among us', just as much as it does, 'All people that on earth do dwell'.

Sometimes this opening music of the liturgy is called 'the Gathering Song', and that indicates at least a part of its function. In most ordinary church communities, it is likely to be something everyone can sing – a hymn or song – for part of what will gather and bind people together is to sing. That, rather than the announcement of a theme, is the function of this hymn. Nevertheless, it is also an important mood-setter. At some times of the year it will be seasonal, but mood is more important. Is this to be a service with a particular air of joy and celebration? Or is a day with a more sober and reflective character? The choice of this first hymn will send out the signal.

This is the point at which to sing the hymns that invite people to join in. 'Enter now his courts with praise' is a good line as a congregation begins to worship and the ministers move towards the sanctuary. It is not so good at a later point. Similarly, 'Come and join the celebration', or, in a different style, 'Come let us join our cheerful songs', are unfortunate when we are about to go home.

Rite A also suggests a 'Sentence'. Very often these should be alternative to, rather than additional to, an opening song. The sentence performs the same function, but without music, of calling to worship and establishing mood. Some of the ASB choices of sentence are unfortunate. They are highly thematic, often didactic, and quite fail to call to worship. 'Be subject for the Lord's sake to every human institution' (1 Peter 2.13) doesn't inspire confidence as the first words the president speaks to the people. Where a thematic sentence is to be used, it needs to follow the greeting and be given some context by a brief word of introduction.

Greeting

'The president welcomes the people.' The first words, save perhaps for a sentence of Scripture as a run-in, that the president addresses to the people are a greeting, which, in its most familiar form, is very simple:

> The Lord be with you
> **and also with you.**

It looks insignificant, but it performs an important function. He greets the people and so, as the Roman instructions rather grandly express it, 'constitutes the assembly'. It is in this exchange that individuals are brought into relationship with him and, through him, with each other. Men, women and children become 'the congregation'.

It is clear, therefore, why it is a presidential text, not delegated to others. It is clear also why its words need to be the first words on his lips. One does not greet someone half way through a conversation, but before the conversation begins. When the president enters, greets the people with a 'Good morning, everyone', announces a hymn, and only five minutes later says, 'The Lord be with you', he has robbed that greeting of its meaning and its function. If he does want to say some less formal words of welcome, they arise naturally out of that more formal liturgical start. They should not precede it.

He addresses this greeting to them from wherever he and the other ministers are to be for the first part of the liturgy, whether around the altar, the lectern or the president's chair.

Rite A provides an alternative form of greeting and also permits other appropriate words. The difficulty with other words is that they confuse the people unless they end 'be with you' and elicit the familiar response, though on special occasions, with printed service orders, this is less of a problem.

Lent, Holy Week, Easter and *The Promise of His Glory* have provided some of the appropriate alternatives:

> Grace, mercy and peace from God our Father
> and the Lord Jesus Christ be with you

> The grace of our Lord Jesus Christ,
> and the love of God,
> and the fellowship of the Holy Spirit
> be with you

> The Lord of glory be with you

and, for All Saintstide,

> May the joy and peace of heaven be with you.

The last two are provided with the response, 'The Lord
bless you', rather than 'and also with you', in an attempt
to move the Church away from a translation of *et cum
spiritu tuo* that many have found unhelpful compared
with the old 'and with thy spirit'. But introducing a
different response to a familiar greeting is difficult.

Care needs to be taken to see that any alternative is
genuinely a greeting. *Patterns for Worship* has a series
of 'Introductions', but they do not have the same sense
of exchange and relationship that the true greeting needs.
That is why Rite A's alternative, 'The Lord is here',
though indisputable, does not work as a greeting. The
Easter greeting, however, for use from Easter Day to
Pentecost, is a fine variant that deserves to be used
consistently through those fifty days.

The formal liturgical greeting over, this is the moment
for the president to set the scene for the celebration.
There may be people to welcome. He may want to give
some indication of theme or intention. Sometimes this
short introduction may itself lead into the Prayers of
Penitence.

The Collect for Purity

This ancient, probably eighth-century prayer, is a well-
established Anglican text, one of those prayers that
many people know by heart. In the past, it was
sometimes pointed out that the Prayer Book service,
that was otherwise deficient in celebrating the role of
the Spirit in the Eucharist, nevertheless began with this
invocation of the Spirit for the whole rite.

Its usefulness is as a warming up and opening up
prayer, helping to draw people into prayerfulness. The
fact that it may be said together, the first prayer said by
all, may also draw people into unity. This might argue
for its use more often at a said celebration, when there

has been no hymn, than when singing has met the same need.

Its use is less obvious when the Prayers of Penitence follow immediately than when they come later in the service. The Preparation can be overdone if everything is included at this point. It may also intrude if the minister wants to use his opening welcome to lead straight into the corporate silent prayer before the collect or into the Prayers of Penitence.

The Prayers of Penitence

Because these may be used at two quite separate points in the service, they are discussed in a chapter of their own (Chapter 10).

Kyrie and Gloria

Both *Kyrie* and *Gloria*, the one known by its Greek name, the other by its Latin, have been in use liturgically since at least the fourth century, though their first use may not have been in the Eucharist.

Kyrie eleison did not at first have the penitential flavour it has now acquired. The meaning was more a matter of 'Lord, show us your favour', and was intercessory in tone. But it is a perfectly legitimate development that it now carries a solemn penitential tone that makes its use appropriate both in seasons like Advent and Lent and also as part of the Prayers of Penitence. In Rite A it is not technically the latter, but its use in this way is discussed in the following chapter.

Alternatively, when the Prayers of Penitence come at the later point in the service, its use at the beginning of the liturgy gives a hint of penitence in our initial approach.

It may be used in many different ways – sixfold, as printed in the main text, threefold or ninefold, in English or in Greek, said or sung. Like the *Gloria* it is as a sung text that its simple repetition is most effective.

The *Gloria*, finding its way into the Eucharist from Morning Prayer (where the ASB has also relocated it), is printed in its normative place in the rite, but it can fit elsewhere. It makes a fine entrance song. The 1662 rite, with its different shape and theology, makes it the crown of the rite before the Blessing, and that can still be done with this rite. Its use is optional, though it is recommended on Sundays, except in Advent and Lent, and on Greater Holy Days. It performs no crucial function in the rite, but carries forward the sense of preparation as the moment draws near to go deeper into prayer.

Many have come to see *Kyrie* and *Gloria* as alternatives, *Gloria* for Sundays (except in Advent and Lent), in Christmastide and Eastertide, and on other holy days, *Kyrie* for Sundays in Advent and Lent and on ordinary 'ferial' weekdays. This is a recent and Anglican way of using them, the one festal, the other penitential, but they serve well in this way, in developing the mood of the celebration. But, for those who wish, both may be used, and both may be omitted.

Bidding, Silent Prayer and The Collect

Everything in the rite between the greeting and the Collect is optional (though the Prayers of Penitence, if omitted here, are mandatory at a later point). The classic start to the eucharistic liturgy is that the president greets the people and invites them to pray. Silence follows as they pray. When they have prayed long enough, and so been drawn deeper into their relationship with God and one another, the liturgy can proceed, its undercurrent of prayerfulness established.

That is the theory, albeit one that is lost to most people. That does not mean that everything that has intervened – Collect for Purity, maybe penitence, *Kyrie*, *Gloria* or even singing of choruses – is superfluous. They have been preparing people for this moment, to go deep into prayer. The sadness is that in most places that idea is so far absent that, when we do reach this point, instead of going deep into prayer, we simply have a collect rattled off by the president, an 'Amen' response, and we sit down. All that warming up to almost no end!

When this point is reached the president must say, 'Let us pray', having taught his people not to regard that as an instruction about posture. If that phrase is too risky, then something like, 'As we stand, let us pray silently together.' Or, looking at the Collect that is to follow, he may want to give that bidding a little more shape, though what he asks people to pray for should not be narrowed down too much or given too definite a direction. This is broad open prayer at the beginning of the liturgy.

In churches where open prayer means something different, members of the congregation praying out loud at the president's bidding, it is appropriate at this point, though the silence must not be squeezed out; and care should be taken to encourage people at this point to major more on prayers of approach, preparation and worship, than on intercession and thanksgiving which will come later.

When the people have prayed sufficiently, the president draws their praying together in the Collect, and the Preparation is now complete.

The Collect is given as the last part of the Preparation, not as the first element of the Ministry of the Word. Nevertheless some of the ASB collects go beyond the convention of being seasonally flavoured, and become straightforwardly thematic, anticipating the readings that are to follow, and its compilers did see its function in these terms. It has happened before, and new Roman Catholic collects are doing the same thing.

Many will regret the passing, in ASB services, of many of the collects of the Prayer Book. Any future revision seems likely to return to the less thematic approach. Meanwhile, at an unofficial level, *Celebrating Common Prayer* (Mowbray 1992), some new proposals for the daily office, gives a set of non-thematic weekly collects, drawing on the best in both Prayer Book and ASB. These may be particularly useful on weekdays, when the readings in any case have no connection with the Sunday theme.

It is intended that there should be only one collect. A string of them makes no sense in this understanding of the collect's function in the rite. One collecting prayer is all that is needed. Where ASB gives more than one for a day, they are alternatives, and one may appropriately be used after communion. Where there are secondary themes to be developed, this is better done in the Prayers of Intercession than by an additional collect here.

10

CONFESSING SIN

An Anglican emphasis

A prominent place for penitence in liturgy has always been part of Anglicanism. The classic expression of it is in the Introduction to Morning and Evening Prayer in the Prayer Book, where the minister says,

> Although we ought at all times humbly to acknowledge our sins before God; yet ought we most chiefly so to do, when we assembly and meet together.

The purists may tell us that corporate penitence at the Eucharist comes late in the tradition (in some ways not until the Middle Ages), but the Anglican instinct has been to recognize its importance. I suppose it is for two reasons. Firstly, we recognize that our sinfulness is part of a fallen world; all sin is, in one sense, corporate, and that needs expression in a general confession we make together. Secondly, we know that the burden of sin, even when we do not realize it, impairs our relationship with God, and that no act of worship is complete without a recognition of that and a desire to put it right.

Prayers of Penitence, therefore, form a significant part of the Eucharist, and as far as regular Sunday worship is concerned it is only when Baptism is to be celebrated that they may be omitted. In practice, however, the tendency in recent years has been to play down the element of penitence in worship. It has been both a reaction to the very full emphasis on it in the Prayer Book, and also a concession to the spirit of the age. It has not been restricted to the Church of England. In the Free Churches an insistence on penitence in worship has been played down in favour of joyful praise.

The truth is, of course, that our praise is, above all else, because we know ourselves penitent sinners who have been forgiven and restored. Perhaps, if we were true to our tradition, we should insist that our liturgies were services of *penitence*, prayer and praise.

What is needed is a recovery of balance. Penitence ought always to be part of our approach to communion, but on occasions it should be brief and to the point, while on other occasions we should be prepared to give more time and space to this element of our worship. But only very rarely should it be omitted altogether.

The place of penitence

In the Church of England we have always been accustomed to the penitential prayers at two different points in worship. In the Prayer Book, penitence in Morning and Evening Prayer comes always at the beginning of the service, in the Eucharist always after the Prayers of Intercession. But it has only been with Holy Communion Rite A that the option has been present to have the Penitential Prayers at the beginning of the rite in the Eucharist also.

One can make sense of either position. If we opt for prayers of penitence at the beginning, we are saying in effect that we cannot come to worship, we cannot relate to our Father in heaven, unless we first put right the relationship that sin has marred. It is as in any human relationship, where a rift needs to be healed before ordinary conversation can be restored. We cannot sing God's praises when we have not yet said sorry. That emphasis points to confession at the very beginning of the liturgy. It is the position that the Roman rite adopts.

If we opt for the later position, after the Intercession and before the Peace, we are taking a rather different view. We say that, if the truth be told, when we come into church we are not worn down with a sense of our sinfulness, the burden is not, in the Prayer Book's words, intolerable. But when we have been there for a while, when we have listened attentively to the Scriptures and the sermon, and when our Prayers of Intercession have reminded us of the mess our world is in, then we are driven to our knees in penitence. It is the liturgy, and supremely the proclamation of God's word, that shows us our need for pardon. If we find that the more convincing argument, we shall opt for penitence at the later point in the rite.

There is a second argument used to support the later point. It draws on Matthew 5.23–4 and the words of the Lord about being reconciled with one another. It sees a connection between penitence and the Greeting of Peace, both being about forgiveness and reconciliation, though the emphasis in the Penitence is above all on our relationship with God and in the Peace with our neighbour.

There is no right or wrong place. Each church needs to decide its norm. For the worship to have rhythm and structure, there needs to be the *normal* place for the Prayers of Penitence. Of course this need not be invariable. When there is a Baptism a church that normally has penitence later might move it to the beginning so that it should not be omitted altogether. On Ash Wednesday a church that normally has penitence at the beginning will recognize the logic of a Liturgy of Penitence after the sermon. But, though not invariable, it will be the norm.

Although it can be extended, when a fuller penitential rite is needed, by one of three additional elements – the Commandments, the Summary of the Law and the 'Comfortable Words' – there are four basic elements to the Prayers of Penitence: an invitation, a time of silence, the confession, the absolution. Silence may be longer or shorter, as circumstances dictate, but cannot be omitted altogether without loss.

The Invitation

'The minister invites the congregation to confess their

sins in these or other suitable words.' Thus the ASB rubric opens up at this point the possibility both of words different from those in the text, and also of a minister other than the president speaking them.

The other suitable words may be 'the Comfortable Words' that give scriptural background to the confession, or one of many texts in circulation, perhaps most often one chosen for its seasonal appropriateness. If the ASB text is used, it should be noted that *Making Women Visible* amends 'live in love and peace with all men' simply to 'live in love and peace'.

But the 'other suitable words' need not be a written text at all. The minister may introduce the confession in his or her own words, and there are certainly occasions when some event will make that personal touch important. As noted above, where the Collect for Purity is omitted, the president will sometimes find that his introduction at the greeting will lead naturally into the Prayers of Penitence.

Nevertheless it may not be the president who speaks at this point. The invitation to confession often falls to the deacon, but it may be any minister.

The Confession

After the Invitation, and at least a pause for sin to be called to mind, the Confession is said. Rite A provides a text, three alternatives in the appendix, and permission to use alternative confessions.

The form in the text and the three in the appendix have the disadvantage of being all rather the same. They are all in the 'Almighty God, our heavenly Father, we have sinned against you . . .' mould. This may well be the standard form, but one might have hoped for different styles among the appendix provisions. The most distinct among them, and the finest composition, is David Frost's 'Father eternal, giver of light and grace . . .' (ASB page 166), which deserves wider use when a weighty confession is needed. In the three of these confessions where the phrase 'against our fellow men' appears, *Making Women Visible* substitutes 'against our neighbour', following the New Testament in understanding 'neighbour' in its widest sense.

Other confessions, outside the ASB, open up other possible styles, and a number are given in *Patterns for Worship*. The Prayer Book confessions (for Morning and Evening Prayer, as well as for the Eucharist) may of course be used, and when a weightier text is required this may meet the need. Care should, however, be taken to choose only confessions that are broad in their embrace. This is a general confession, where people bring a whole variety of sins for forgiveness. They are not served by a confession that narrows their sin down to pride or environmental pollution or lack of faith.

One of the other styles of confession, specially suitable when the Penitence is at the beginning and needs to be quite brief, is the use of the *Kyries. Lent, Holy Week, Easter* first introduced these to Church of England worship, though they were known as one of the penitential options in the Roman rite. One of the *Lent, Holy Week, Easter* texts is this:

> You raise the dead to life in the Spirit:
> Lord, have mercy.
> **Lord, have mercy.**
>
> You bring pardon and peace to sinners:
> Christ, have mercy.
> **Christ, have mercy.**
>
> You bring light to those in darkness:
> Lord, have mercy.
> **Lord, have mercy.**

Enriching the Christian Year gives a whole series of seasonal penitential *Kyries. Patterns for Worship* spells out how they are to be constructed:

Sentences may be inserted between the petitions of the Kyrie, to add depth to the penitential section at particular seasons, for example Lent, or on occasions to act as a substitute for confession. In the latter case, the sentences should be of a penitential character . . .

The sentences should in any case be short. They may well follow the theme of the readings and opening greeting, and be trinitarian in style.

If there has not been a significant time of silence after the Invitation, there need to be silences between the sentences of the *Kyries* to allow time for each individual to express specific penitence for sin.

The Absolution

Absolutions are carefully protected in the Church of England because the whole business of pronouncing God's forgiveness has been a doctrinally sensitive question. The rite, therefore, allows no alternatives or variations at this point. But some variants have been proposed in *Patterns for Worship*.

Earlier books, commended by the House of Bishops, have permitted:

> May almighty God have mercy on us,
> forgive us our sins,
> and bring us to everlasting life.

This form is particularly designed to follow the penitential *Kyries*, the style of which calls for a short, sharp ending.

The Prayer Book's fuller absolution, in an amended form, was commended by the House of Bishops in *Lent, Holy Week, Easter*:

> Almighty God, our heavenly Father,
> who of his great mercy has promised forgiveness of sins
> to all those who with heartfelt repentance and true faith turn to him:
> have mercy upon *you*,

pardon and deliver *you* from all *your* sins,
confirm and strengthen *you* in all goodness,
and bring *you* to the joy of heaven;
through Jesus Christ our Lord.

The italicizing of *you* and *your* in absolutions is not entirely because of their use by deacons and lay people in the absence of a priest, though that is one reason. There is the option even for bishops and priests to use the more inclusive *us* form, which is what is found in the Roman rite, though the *you* form has always been the Church of England custom.

Although no rubric indicates it, it is an established and appropriate mark of the absolution for the president to make the sign of the cross over the people as he says 'pardon and deliver you from all your sins'. It is a reminder that our forgiveness is because of the sacrifice of Christ upon the cross. When this sign is used, it needs to be a bold and strong gesture if it is to witness to the power of the cross.

11

HEARING THE LIVELY WORD

The word proclaimed

In the Prayer Book Communion rite, prayer is offered for bishops and curates,

> that they may both by their life and doctrine set forth thy true and lively Word, and rightly and duly administer thy holy Sacraments.

It is the word, as well as the sacrifice, that is to be *lively*, and, although the meaning, of course, is primarily that it is to be living in the sense that Christ speaks to us through it, it needs to be proclaimed with the kind of sensitivity and conviction that is lively in the other sense too. The Scriptures are good news, and they need to be proclaimed and heard with clarity, with joy and with awe. If they are read as God's word for his people, if Christ is present among his people in the reading of Scripture, the atmosphere has to be one of expectation. People should expect to hear a message for their lives.

The service up to this point has prepared them for this moment. They have been led to the point where they are ready to pray deeply. In that prayer they have been opened up to God and the action of his Spirit. Now they sit to hear the Scriptures. What a responsibility for those who now come to the lectern!

Just as the quotation from the Prayer Book gives an equality to setting forth the word and administering the sacraments, so it is important that the Eucharist be seen as a service of both word and sacrament. People sometimes make something of the fact that it is in reality two services merged into one – a word service and a meal – but the remarkable thing is that the two have been held together for more than fifteen hundred years. The Church in her wisdom has seen that the two should remain merged. But the problem has sometimes been that the word can look as if it is simply part of the preparation for the sacrament. It is more than that.

The Prayer Book Communion rite contributed to this, with its word element reduced to two often quite short readings with no psalmody or canticle material. In theory there was always a sermon, but not often in practice. This did not matter when people were receiving a richer diet of Scripture at Morning and Evening Prayer, but very often the Communion was the only service to which they went. Part of what we have to recover, and the Rite A rubrics encourage it, is the sense that the word is not a mere preliminary, but a major part of the rite, with its own internal shape and climax.

Three readings are regarded as the norm. This must be right at the Sunday liturgy when this is the one service most people will attend during the week. There are difficulties nevertheless. One is that the ASB lectionary readings are quite long, longer than the equivalent in the three-year 'common lectionary' that is gaining wider acceptance. The ASB recognizes that its provision is very full, and allows for only two readings, one of which is always the Gospel, the other of which is the Old Testament reading in the run-up to Christmas, the epistle reading from Pentecost onwards, and either for the rest of the year. In practice this seems to have meant in most churches the use of the epistle option nearly all of the time to the neglect of the Old Testament.

Detailed lectionary considerations go beyond the scope of this book. There is a basic divergence of approach between those who advocate the ASB sort of lectionary, thematic in style, and those who prefer the 'common lectionary' approach, with its semi-continuous reading of biblical books, its concern for season but not for theme, and the centrality it gives in each of its three years to just one of the synoptic Gospels.

But, whatever lectionary is used, a new freedom needs

to be sought. It ought to be permissible for a parish to break away from the lectionary at certain neutral periods of ordinary time in the Christian year. Both *The Promise of His Glory* and *Patterns for Worship* have provided lectionary material that would allow a church to employ units of Scripture over a number of weeks that would widen their exposure to the Bible and also fit the particular needs of that community in its Christian development. Such a freedom should be resisted for the parts of the Christian year where the liturgical cycle is at its most powerful, but what is needed is a recognition that there are 'closed' and 'open' seasons as far as lectionary provision is concerned.

A freedom like this would also allow a parish to read in the liturgy some of the great Old Testament sagas that lose half their impact when divided up into lection-sized extracts. The story of Noah and the flood, for instance, or the Book of Ruth, could simply take over the Ministry of the Word for a day, with perhaps just a short Gospel to provide Christian 'comment', though there would be much work to be done in ensuring that the story was presented in such a way that attention was held. The tale would need to be well told, probably not by a single voice from the lectern. *The Dramatised Bible* (Marshall Pickering/Bible Society 1989) is a very fine resource.

For, though we speak of 'reading' the lessons, and though a single voice at the lectern proclaiming the Scriptures audibly and meaningfully remains the norm, there are so many other ways that the word can be made lively, whether it be by dramatized reading, by the use of lighting, by mime or by the employment of song.

The readers of the Scriptures

It is part of the ministry of lay people, coming out of the congregation, to read the Old Testament and epistle readings. Readers should be chosen for their ability to be heard and to communicate the meaning of the reading effectively. The reading of these lessons should not be taken over by the clergy (see Chapter 2).

The tradition assigns the Gospel reading to the deacon (see Chapter 4), and where there is a deacon of the Eucharist, he or she will obviously fulfil this function. Where there is no deacon, Anglican provision does not specify who reads the Gospel. In some churches only a priest reads the Gospel, but the only logic of this tradition is that he is doing so because he is also a deacon. It is perfectly proper for a lay person to proclaim the gospel. In some places the desire to reserve it to an ordained minister is simply to enhance its significance as the high point of this part of the liturgy, but this can also be achieved in other ways.

Alternatively there is an argument, in the absence of a deacon, for the Gospel to be read by the preacher, especially if the Gospel is read and the sermon preached from the same place.

The significance of the Gospel is sometimes signalled by the deacon receiving a blessing from the president before reading it. Usually under cover of the pre-gospel song, the deacon bows to receive a blessing such as this:

> The Lord be in your heart and on your lips that you may worthily proclaim his holy Gospel; in the name of the Father, and of the Son, and of the Holy Spirit.

Despite a common misunderstanding, it is the deacon, not the gospel book, that is blessed. Indeed if the lectionary is already on the lectern the deacon will not be holding it at the time of the blessing.

The Gospel is sometimes preceded by the traditional salutation:

> The Lord be with you
> **and also with you**.

The logic of this is that it is the deacon's greeting before addressing the people for the first time. There is less sense in it when spoken by a president who has exchanged the same greeting with the people a few minutes before, or if the deacon has already given the notices or introduced the confession.

Mention has already been made of the desirability of proclaiming the Scriptures from one significant place using one large and sturdy book of the Scriptures. The Gospel may be highlighted by candles, by the Acclamations (sung or said) that greet it, and by the whole congregation standing and turning towards its proclamation. The further custom of a procession, to read it in the midst of the people (with or without the turning north to face the heathen!), goes back twelve hundred years and gives the Gospel its special place, but questions of audibility and visibility need to be faced. The important thing is that the gospel should be effectively proclaimed and received.

Between the readings

Psalms, canticles and hymns are encouraged between the readings. Certainly, quite apart from the desirability of using the rich treasury of Christian song, there needs to be something between the readings. One reading after the other without pause is never the way; there needs to be space for assimilation. Silence may provide this, but so may song.

The near disappearance of the psalter from the worship experience of those who attend only the Eucharist is very worrying. A Christianity that is not fed on the psalms will be an impoverished thing. This need not mean Anglican chant week by week, for there are so many other ways to sing the psalms, but if none of these seems accessible in a particular congregation, let some verses of psalm at least be *said*.

One fashion is for a responsorial psalm. A reader (probably the same reader who has read the Old Testament lesson) reads the text, the people make a repeated response, sufficiently short and immediately memorable for them not to need a printed text. This is effective, and it is not beyond any minister's devising to choose a line from the psalms set in ASB to provide the response.

But a word of defence may be given for the saying of the psalm in the form traditional for Morning and Evening Prayer, with the verses alternating either between minister and people, or from side to side in the church. The former allows more control to be exercised by a leader and prevents the psalm gathering speed or growing too much in volume. Although this style has seemed to belong more to the office than to the Eucharist, it enables people to enter more obviously into the rhythm of the psalms, which is an important part of how they communicate.

Whether it be at the main Sunday liturgy or on a weekday, cannot a portion of psalmody follow the first reading? Usually it would be used seated, reflectively, though some psalms of praise demand a different posture.

An alternative to psalmody is the rich canticle material now available. Much of it draws on the Old Testament, and that is what fits best after an Old Testament reading. Most of the canticles now available in, for instance, *The Promise of His Glory* and *Enriching the Christian Year*, have a response printed, so that they too can be used responsorially and without a text for the entire congregation.

Between the epistle and gospel readings a New Testament or other Christian song is appropriate. If it is a hymn, it needs to be chosen for its suitability to this point in the liturgy, probably the most thematic hymn, picking up on the readings that precede or follow it, but quite brief. It needs to maintain the impetus towards the Gospel, rather than be a stage of the service in its own right.

It is a long-established custom to prepare for the Gospel with a burst of Alleluias around a sentence of Scripture. The Roman rite has these, and the music is available, though inevitably these are linked to the Roman calendar and lectionary. But a well-chosen Alleluia hymn, chant or song often sets the mood for the Gospel – though not in Lent.

The sermon

The sermon follows the Gospel because it ought to be grounded in the Scriptures that have preceded it. Styles of sermon will vary, but where there is no sense in which the preaching arises from what has gone before, something important is lost.

All Church of England rites indicate that the sermon is mandatory. It is not a matter of a sermon '*may* be preached', though a Rite A note softens the provision by insisting that there be a sermon at every Eucharist only on Sundays and Holy Days. 'The sermon', it insists, 'is an integral part of the Ministry of the Word.'

One of the arts that those who lead worship need to acquire is the ability to pick up on a phrase in the readings and draws out its meaning and relevance in just a few sentences. It is more of a thought for the day, than a sermon as we have understood that word; or sometimes we speak of it as a homily, which somehow seems less heavy than a sermon. This would meet the need on weekdays and at a Sunday early celebration.

In the Sunday Eucharist, preachers sometimes want to give the message a less intimidating tone, or to justify a very different sort of style from usual, and so at this point comes 'The Talk' rather than 'The Sermon'. There is a lot to be said for staying with the traditional terms 'preaching' and 'sermon'. I think my expectation of a talk is less than my expectation of a good sermon! But that does not mean that for every occasion 'sermon' will mean the same thing. It may be sometimes the thought for the day approach, sometimes a well developed fifteen-minute sermon of the traditional Anglican kind, sometimes a teaching experience with overhead projector, sometimes a dividing into groups for study, sometimes a dramatic presentation, but if, whichever it is, we still call it 'The Sermon', we shall be reminded that, in whatever form, its purpose is to preach the good news of Christ and to do so partly by expounding the Scriptures. Under a variety of guises there always needs to be a sermon preached.

The Creed

The Nicene Creed follows the sermon, at least on Sundays and Holy Days, as the people's response to the reading and preaching. It is one of the points where clergy have found the Rite A provision constricting, for it is a difficult text to use, especially in a congregation of which children are a part. *Patterns for Worship* proposes some other scriptural 'Affirmations of Faith' for use on occasions, though it would be wrong to see the Nicene Creed disappear. It is a part of our tradition with which people need to remain familiar. That is different from saying that it needs to be used every Sunday.

Part of the problem has come in the fashion for saying, rather than singing, it. The purists have maintained that, whereas the *Gloria* is a song of praise and should therefore be sung, the Creed is a statement of faith and should therefore be said. But this is a false distinction, and doctrine in worship always needs to turn into doxology. When the Creed is sung, it does not lose its doctrinal content, but it does become a great outburst of praise. When it is said, it can seem long and turgid, and to be ploughed through as a duty. The affirmation of Christian faith should not be like that. Composers should set to work.

The custom of turning east (and it is east, rather than to the altar) for the Creed owes something to the Creed's origin as a baptismal profession of faith. Candidates turned to the west, where the sun sets, to renounce evil, and to the east, where the sun rises, to make their profession of faith. It is an obscure bit of symbolism for most people today, and seems odd when it involves choir or other ministers turning their backs on the sanctuary.

The Notices

An ASB note suggests that the Notices may follow the Creed. If they are placed here, they need to strike a note that makes them a natural lead into the Prayers of Intercession. We learn what is to happen in the coming week, and then we pray about it. There is no better place within the service, though some will still prefer the option of pre-service notices, and others their insertion just before the Dismissal.

12

INTERCEDING BROADLY

The Prayers of the People

Intercession is a natural response to the reading and preaching of God's word. This is one of the points in the service where the undercurrent of prayer comes to the surface, and this time the prayers have an intercessory flavour. Rite A's reference to prayers 'of intercession and thanksgiving' is unfortunate, for, though prayer cannot be tightly compartmentalized, it is intercession that is the concern now, and thanksgiving has its natural place as it is caught up in the praises of the Eucharistic Prayer a little later on. Obviously there will be thanksgiving at this point, but it ought to be of a sort that leads quickly into intercession.

These prayers have traditionally been called 'The Prayers of the Faithful' or 'of the People', and that sense needs preserving. It is not *necessarily* about who leads them, but about who prays them, and all that has been said about praying when all is silent and still applies very strongly here. Nevertheless, the growing custom that these prayers are led by lay people is a good one. Sometimes the fact that these are the people's prayers is expressed also by the fact that they are led from the midst of the people, and that is fine provided they are audible. The people's prayers need to be heard, even if that means that they are led from the lectern.

There is also a tradition that involves the deacon in the Prayers of Intercession, and there may still be a place for this. Using this approach, the deacon gives the biddings, in a sense 'sets the agenda', but often this means articulating prayers that individuals have requested, perhaps collecting them up at the door before the service. This is a different way of ensuring that the prayers are 'the people's'.

The role of the president is simply to draw it all together, whether once at the end, or repeatedly section by section through the prayer.

Each community needs to develop its normal style and, in so doing, to think through the way it involves the president, the deacon and the people. Traditions do not need to be adhered to, but the principle that the people are being given the material and the space to pray is fundamental.

If the Prayers of Intercession are to provide the setting for the people's prayers they need to retain a broad sweep. There are services where intercession rightly focuses on a few precise and defined areas. But the Eucharist is not like that. It has to encompass everything that people bring to prayer. There will always be somebody present who is feeling deeply about some atrocity or sadness in the world, somebody with an urgent prayer for a sick neighbour or a friend in trouble, somebody for whom it is the anniversary of the death of somebody dear. If the Prayers of Intercession are too narrowly focused, these needs will not find their place. Although the Rite A Intercession shape, with its five sections – Church, World, Local Community, Those in Need, The Departed – can grow stale and lifeless, at least it ensures that the prayer remains broad, and the Eucharist the setting for offering to God the whole of his creation.

For this reason, there ought to be a reluctance to omit the Prayers of Intercession at any Eucharist. Even when there has been Baptism, Confirmation or any other special rite between the sermon and the Greeting of Peace, Intercession should, if possible, be inserted, however succinctly.

There is one issue on which those who lead inter-cession often seem unclear, and it is helpful to clarify it. To whom are the prayers addressed? If they are genuinely prayers, they must be addressed to God. If they are biddings ('Let us pray for . . .') they are addressed to the people, inviting them to do the praying. All too often Prayers of Intercession confuse these two forms. The use of the ASB's

> Almighty God, our heavenly Father, you promised through your Son Jesus Christ, to hear us when we pray in faith

commits the leader from the outset to the 'prayer' approach, directing all the words to God, with no room for a 'Let us pray for . . .'. But the bidding approach is a legitimate alternative, and the one that preserves more clearly the truth that it is the people who pray; the leader simply sets the agenda.

Styles of intercession

Rite A permits a great variety of approach to the style of intercession. It provides one complete text in the mainstream rite, though even this can be used in more than one way, but then adds two alternatives in an appendix, and then permission to use 'other suitable words'. It is a wide freedom.

It needs to be used wisely. A church needs to guard against the twin dangers of, on the one hand, having no pattern or norm to its intercessory prayer, so that every occasion is an experiment, and the prayer is over before most people have discovered its shape, and, on the other hand, a bored predictability that can take hold of the Prayers of Intercession. There needs to be variety and freshness, if these prayers are to be alive, but some local norms and conventions can help a church make more of this prayer time. In this section we examine the various styles that can be employed.

The mainstream text at section 21 of Rite A most obviously invites a style addressed to God throughout, moving through five areas of concern, with local material inserted between a set text. Each of its five sections (excluding the concluding formula) would have four elements:

1. Leader's material, sometimes extempore, addressed to God
2. Silence for the people to add and to make the prayer their own
3. A Response: 'Lord, in your mercy
   Hear our prayer.'
4. A set summing up paragraph ('Strengthen N our bishop . . .' etc.)

There are two immediate variations on this:

The first is to reverse 3 and 4. Using 4 last gives it the character of the concluding collect to each section, perhaps spoken by a different minister. Reversing 3 and 4 makes leader's material and set text more of a piece.

The second is to remove the prayer's opening sentence ('Almighty God, our heavenly Father, you promised through your Son Jesus Christ . . .') so that God has not been addressed, and the leader can instead make biddings addressed to the people. In this shape, 1 becomes in each case an agenda-setting for the people, 2 becomes the substance of the people's prayer, and 4 becomes a collecting prayer addressed to God.

With any of these uses, leaders should note two possible textual changes to the ASB text. *Making Women Visible* amends 'men may honour one another' to 'we may honour one another'. In the concluding formula, ASB's 'all Christian people' is an unfortunate narrowing down where the prayer ought to be at its most inclusive. 'We commend ourselves and your whole creation' is infinitely preferable.

Another style, similar to those above, simply omits 4, the concluding prayer of each section, and has a repeated cycle of:

1. leader's material
2. silent prayer
3. response.

The conclusion is a single one at the end of the whole cycle of intercession.

But there is another quite different model of intercession that is established in the Anglican tradition, and which is reconcilable with the text on ASB page 125. It is the model of extended biddings followed by set text without interpolation. This is the style people adopt with the Prayer Book. Before reading the Prayer 'for the whole state of Christ's Church', the minister gives the congregation a number of prayer intentions or topics, but then reads the prayer without interruption.

The disadvantages of this style as a norm are clear. The most obvious is that there is little sense of the people's prayer, except in keeping up with the minister, because there are many words and few silences. A second disadvantage is that the people have to hold together all the ideas for prayer at one time, rather than coming to them in some sort of logical order section by section. But the advantage is that two very different styles of language are being kept apart, first the minister's probably very direct extempore spontaneous words, and then the formal words of the liturgy that are often too carefully constructed to cope with much interpolation. Certainly this is so with the Prayer Book's Prayer for the Church, which in style cannot sustain intrusions ('especially we pray today for . . .') without a sad loss of rhythm and poetry that itself engenders prayer.

In the range of intercession styles that churches use, the form of bidding followed by set prayer without interpolation ought to have a place. It has a number of uses:

It can be used with the Rite A text as it stands.

It can be used to rehabilitate in modern liturgy texts like the Prayer Book Prayer for the Church and the modification of it in Rite B.

It can be used with litanies, and in particular with the fine Litany in the Rite A appendix. Litanies, with their oft repeated congregational response, are, of all forms, the tightest rhythmical construction, where inter-polation destroys the flow.

It can be used for seasonal intercessions. Recent books, notably *Enriching the Christian Year*, provide intercession forms closely tied to the particular character of different festivals and seasons. Some of these invite interpolation, but the majority are better treated as liturgical compositions with their own integrity, and local material in the form of biddings given first before the prayer begins.

Then there is opportunity to be much less structured, to have, in effect, a time of 'open' or 'free' prayer. Those who are at home in this style know its difficulties in a large assembly, especially in terms of audibility, and also that, for all its openness and freedom, it needs organizing and holding together. Whether it be the spoken extempore prayer of a single voice, or an occasion when many will contribute out loud, it fulfils the brief of 'other suitable prayer' providing there is the breadth to the content and sufficient space between the words for everybody to feel that their prayer has a place within it.

There is a new growing understanding of the place of music in intercession, both through the sung response and the use of song as a background to silent prayer. This is explored briefly in Chapter 22.

In the end, whatever forms are used, and whether they follow the conventions or break all the rules, the fundamental truth to hold on to is that these are the people's prayers, and the praying probably begins when the leader stops talking.

The Prayer of Humble Access

When the Prayers of Penitence have been used earlier in the service, the Prayers of the People lead very naturally into the Greeting of Peace. But in Rite A there is an intrusion, albeit an optional one. It is Cranmer's Prayer of Humble Access, originally composed in 1549 for the penitential prayers immediately prior to communion, but which has since found a variety of places in Anglican rites.

It is a fine prayer, one of the valued texts from the Prayer Book tradition, now set alongside a fine alternative by David Frost, already discussed ('Most merciful Lord, your love compels us to come in . . .') in the appendix. The problem is that, fine as it is, there is no right place for it. Wherever it is placed, it interrupts the flow of the liturgy. Its continued use is evidence that pastoral sensitivity often outweighs liturgical purity.

13

MAKING PEACE

In love and charity

In the place that Rite A assigns to it, the same place that it has in Justin Martyr's second-century description of the Eucharist, the Peace has a pivotal role in the liturgy, and marks the transition from word to sacrament.

It concludes the Ministry of the Word in the sense that it is the seal either of the Prayers of the People or of the Prayers of Penitence, both of which lead very naturally into it. It looks forward to the Ministry of the Sacrament, first of all in being a ritualizing of the command of Jesus to be reconciled to our neighbour before bringing our gift to the altar, and also in being, in effect, the opening greeting of this second service.

The Prayer Book Communion rite includes the invitation:

Ye that do truly and earnestly repent you of your sins, and are in love and charity with your neighbours . . . . Draw near . . . and take this Holy Sacrament to your comfort . . .

and the Peace attempts to express something of the same sense in which the communicants must be reconciled to their neighbours before they bring their gifts and share around the altar table.

The two sets of words that the ASB provides to introduce the Peace wear thin with over-use, for, like every symbolic gesture, the Peace is better without too much explanation. But the two texts do underline truths that the Peace is trying to convey.

One is about reconciliation: 'He has reconciled us to God in one body by the cross.' And reconciliation, though it begins with Christ and his sacrifice, extends out into our relationships one with another. It means being 'in love and charity with your neighbour', with 'neighbour' used in that broad and inclusive way that Jesus adopted. In the sign of Peace, those sharing in the Eucharist express not only their love and charity for those present there with them in the celebration (though that is sometimes a painful and demanding thing), but symbolically the reconciliation of the whole of humankind in Christ. When the Peace follows the Prayers, with their emphasis on the world and its sorrows, that can become very clear.

But the words of Paul that 'we are the Body of Christ' and that, as such, we are to build up our common life, are saying something equally important, this time about the Church. Paul's fascinating phrase in 1 Corinthians 11 about 'discerning the body' in the Lord's Supper signals a theology that reflects on the relationship between 'being the body' and 'eating the body'. Our reconciliation, our love and charity, though they are about our common humanity, are also about our being in Christ, and we affirm something very awesome as we greet one another immediately before we remember the death and resurrection of the Lord.

This may all be true, but why, people sometimes ask, does this now need to be expressed more overtly than in the past? In the Prayer Book, for instance, it was there, but in a much more subtle way. The answer is partly to do with the change in the nature of communities. In the past the Church reflected a community life that was natural, settled and clear for all to see. It is still just about discernible in some villages, though even they have changed their character a good deal. But most people live in a modern urban or suburban world in which any sense of community is difficult to establish, and many who come to church relate to one another for worship on a Sunday but are part of different levels of community through the week. Here, if the congregation is to be the Body of Christ, and to be drawn into love and charity, the Church is more in the business of 'community creation' than 'community maintenance'. Relationships cannot be taken for granted; they need to be made. The Greeting of Peace is a part of that process.

The sign of peace

So how is this Greeting to be given? Firstly the people need to be standing, as the rubric directs. Even in a community where there is to be no 'passing' of the Peace, simply the words between president and people, there must be a consciousness of the community and a sense that we are talking to one another, and this is not achieved with the people on their knees.

The president introduces the Peace. He may not need a sentence of Scripture, as provided in the text. The only lead in may be, 'My brothers and my sisters, the peace of the Lord . . . .' But, if he does want a sentence to set the scene and give a kind of biblical warrant, in addition to the two in the text, and the five in the appendix, all the recent books have provided seasonal introductions for every occasion.

Where there is the ministry of a deacon, it is sometimes the deacon's, rather than the president's, task to say, 'Let us offer one another a sign of peace.'

What then happens must vary from one community to another. What does not work is a passing *down* of the Peace whereby the president greets those in the sanctuary, who 'take' it to the people row by row, so that it eventually reaches those at the back after a long wait. By then it has gone cold, so to speak. The invitation to offer one another a sign of peace must be taken up in the congregation immediately with people greeting those around them, but being careful not to greet only their friends. The ministers, if possible, move among the people.

There is no need for many words between people. 'Peace be with you', or 'The peace of Christ', is quite sufficient. In some communities there will no doubt be hugs and kisses, but they can be rather exclusive (when restricted to friends) as well as intimidating (when extended to strangers), and the shy English smile with hesitant handshake or handclasp will be more appropriate in most places.

For restraint is not out of place, and not only because people may not be able to cope. It is appropriate because what is being affirmed is an awesome thing. Being the Body of Christ, being in love and charity with your neighbour, being reconciled through Christ, are none of them light and cheery things. There is a proper reticence to the way we express them, though how reticent will depend on the kind of people we are.

Restraint is important also because the momentum of the service must not be lost at this point. We are embarking on something. The Peace begins the Ministry of the Sacrament and must propel us on into that. It is a lovely and significant moment in the liturgy; but at another level it is only a preliminary to what is to come.

Another place: another meaning

Note 20 allows the Peace to be moved to another point in the service. People sometimes argue for it to be placed at the beginning, in a sense strengthening the opening greeting. The difficulty with that position is that it gives the Peace the function of being a welcoming rite – people are asked to turn to those whom they don't know and greet them – and that may be good, but it is losing the emphasis on reconciliation and on the Body of Christ.

A better case can be made for a position, adopted by the Roman rite, at the Breaking of the Bread. Here it becomes the people's assent to the Eucharistic Prayer, draws the sense of reconciliation close to the words of the Lord's Prayer ('Forgive us our trespasses, as we forgive those who trespass against us') and of the *Agnus Dei* ('Grant us peace'), and also retains the body imagery as it associates the Peace with the breaking of bread ('We break this bread to share in the body of Christ').

The difficulty with this position is that any moving around to greet one another at that point immediately before communion, does cut across the momentum of the rite, and seems an intrusion at a point when the communicant is preparing to receive. It is difficult to see that it is a better place than the pivotal point which Rite A gives it.

14

OFFERING GIFTS

Preparing and offering

The next part of the service is one that, in some churches, is as rich in movement and ritual as any. In a fine procession in which bread and wine are brought to the altar, and even incense is used, one of the high points of the liturgy is reached. It is precisely the 'success' of such a presentation that has worried liturgists and theologians, and their worries are reflected in some hesitant and confusing instructions in Rite A, Sections 32 to 36. That in turn has created the kind of misunderstandings that, in other churches, have made this one of the least satisfactory points in the service.

The confusion begins with the name. Rite A carefully never uses the word 'offertory' to describe this stage of the service. There is 'preparation' and later 'taking', but not 'offertory'. Yet most churchpeople do have 'offertory' in their vocabulary. By it they mean the bringing to the altar of bread and wine. Sometimes they think of it as including also the collection and presentation of money. And indeed some of them mean just that and nothing else. The use of the word 'offertory' in the Prayer Book Communion service is ambiguous, but certainly seems to include the money as definitely as anything else.

The ASB has not omitted the word 'offertory' only because it has become hopelessly muddled. It does so out of deference to those for whom it presents a theological problem. It is part of that same Evangelical sensitivity that is suspicious that in the way some people use the words 'sacrifice', 'offering' and 'oblation' they are undermining the uniqueness of Christ's offering of himself upon the cross. They suspect unacceptable doctrine.

It is that sensitivity that accounts also for the strangest rubric in the rite. Section 33 reads:

> The president may praise God for his gifts in appropriate words to which all respond,
> **Blessed be God for ever**.

The rubric is intended to permit the Roman offertory prayers ('Blessed are you, Lord God of creation, through your goodness we have this bread to offer . . .'), based on Jewish meal graces, for those who find them attractive, yet not to print them, because of their use of the language of 'offering'.

The offertory procession

The doubts and confusions become deeper when we consider the common practice of bringing the bread and wine to the altar, not in a straightforward and practical way from the credence table the short distance to the altar, but in procession from the back of the church, the 'elements' (sometimes including also the water to be mixed with the wine) being carried by members of the congregation, and the procession led sometimes by the cross and lights, and even the ministers who go down to lead them up.

Offertory processions predate the 1960s' liturgical reforms. They began as an attempt to relate liturgy and life through affirming that in the Eucharist we bring to God symbols of our human work, and it is these that he takes and uses in the Eucharist, transforming them and giving them back to us. The emphasis is on offering the work of human hands, a theme reflected in the Roman offertory prayers. Sometimes the symbolism is developed further, so that bread becomes the sign of work, of labour, sometimes even of pain, but wine the sign of festivity, celebration, the other side of life, though that has always had its difficulty when the wine is to become for us the blood shed for the forgiveness of sins.

In the post-war years, when the offertory procession first became the fashion (with the Prayer Book Communion rite), it was not of course a novelty, but a return to early practice, when people did actually bring their own loaves to the Eucharist, some of which were used for the celebration, while the others went to feed the hungry. As the custom was revived, it sometimes meant putting one's own wafer (provided by the church) into the ciborium near the door. This was not (at least originally) a practicality about getting the numbers right, but a theological statement about the offering of one's life and labour to God. The money came to be associated with the same procession, because it was recognized that it was in that, as much as in the bread and wine, that we express the giving of our daily life to God.

It is important to realize that the practice caught on, and is still retained in a very large number of churches, because people recognized in it something important that they were trying to express. Their daily lives and their Sunday worship were and are related. The Eucharist was and is not a narrow churchy thing, but a bringing to God of the whole of his creation. There was and is an instinct that this ritual says something worth saying.

But there have always been those (Archbishop Michael Ramsey among them) who were alarmed at this sort of emphasis. We come to the Eucharist with nothing.

> Just as I am, without one plea
> but that thy blood was shed for me.

We come to God, empty, hungry, needing to be fed. He gives us richly, and his giving is not in response to ours. Everything is his initiative and his grace.

This is another paradox of the Eucharist. At one level we can and do bring nothing. God does not need our gift. He is not dependent on us. And, at one level, all that matters is the offering of Christ upon the cross, and the way that the Eucharist renews his death and life within us. And yet our love for God is what makes us approach him wanting to offer, to give. It is the knowledge of the sacrifice of Christ that creates in us the yearning to consecrate our lives and the life of our world, and so, in a sense, to lay them on the altar.

There is both the danger that the very word 'offertory' will lead to false doctrine, and also the further danger that an offertory procession could compound the error. These dangers must make us cautious. Nevertheless, provided that we see the preparation of the gifts as essentially preliminary, preparatory, to what God does in the sacrament, there are deeply Christian instincts in celebrating and ritualizing this sense of bringing to God all that needs his touch.

To keep these truths in the right proportion we need to ensure that we do not make the offertory, if we call it that, a high point of the liturgy. We may have a procession, but it needs to be restrained. It must not say too much. The words that accompany it, if there are to be any, must not claim too much. Something important is being expressed, but something infinitely more important is still to come.

The four actions

There is one other area of thinking that has contributed to the confusion. It relates to the four actions of Christ in the Last Supper, that appear also in the New Testament in other descriptions of meals that have a eucharistic character to them. Jesus takes, gives thanks, breaks, gives. The Church does these four things in every Eucharist – taking, giving thanks, breaking, giving. Whereas in the Prayer Book Communion rite, the four are drawn together as far as possible into a single moment of time, eucharistic rites usually draw them out and reflect on each in turn, finding in each deep meaning and symbolism. Or that, at least, is the assumption on which a good deal of liturgical reform, and teaching in parishes, has proceeded (but see also the following chapter).

Two insights follow from this. The first is that *words* about the bread and wine belong in the Eucharistic Prayer. They are part of the 'giving thanks'. It confuses the issue to praise God for them and celebrate their meaning in a kind of mini-eucharistic prayer at an earlier point. The liturgists see no point in a text for the preparation. It is best done in silence. Thus there are no mandatory words in this section of the service.

The second is that the 'preparing', or the offertory, is not to be identified with the 'taking', in the way that people have often done. People have built this rich symbolism into the offertory, and have believed that in so doing they were building on the first of the Lord's four actions, the taking. But we now know that 'taking' was not the practical business of laying the table, but a simple symbolic gesture, emerging from Jewish practice, whereby the president, when the table laying was over, lifted the bread and wine a few inches above the table in silence and then replaced them, thus indicating, before he began the prayer, the bread and wine over which thanks were to be given.

The taking is, on this view, not the offertory at all, but something that follows it, and this is what the mandatory Rite A rubric at section 36,

> The president takes the bread and cup into his hands and replaces them on the holy table

is expecting. Yet this rubric is rarely understood and even more rarely followed. In the popular mind preparation, offertory and taking are all mixed up together. This may well be a misreading of the history of the rite, but it may also be a recognition that, by being identified with preparation and offertory, 'taking' has found some meaning.

Laying the table

With all this in the background, it is helpful now to look at what Rite A says at this point, and how it may best be used in a way that signals as little confusion as possible.

In Section 32, which is mandatory, the instruction is given that the bread and wine are placed on the table. This may be a simple movement of chalice and paten, already prepared, from the credence table to the altar, or it may mean an element of procession. If the latter, all that has gone before suggests that this should be a simple procession of members of the congregation, bringing bread, wine and water, without too much fuss and ceremony, to the president or deacon, probably while a hymn is being sung. What sort of bread they bring will be discussed later (in Chapter 16), but it ought to be capable of being broken for sharing, and therefore the practice of everyone putting a wafer in the ciborium at the door (or worse somebody sitting there doing it for them) should not feature.

But whether it is the simplest practical placing on the table or something a little more symbolic and elaborate, this is the point to lay the table. It is best if until this point the altar is free of bread and cup. The focus until this point has been the Ministry of the Word. Churches that follow a tradition going back to 1552, and permitted in Note 20, of laying the table before the service might think again.

If there is an argument for a procession at this point, it is strengthened by the desire to parallel the processional bringing in of the Scriptures at the beginning of the rite. The bringing of bread and wine to the altar now marks the transition from word to sacrament.

The minister of this table-laying is by tradition the deacon. Where the deacon does undertake this, the president is set free to sit quietly and prepare himself for the Eucharistic Prayer.

The minister, whether president or deacon, makes ready the table. Sufficient bread and wine are placed centrally upon it. If it is possible to have just one paten or ciborium and just one chalice (perhaps with a flagon of additional wine), the sense of unity of the sacrament is enhanced. At the fraction the bread can be broken on to several 'plates' and the wine poured into several chalices, but the visual impact of 'one bread and one cup' through the Eucharistic Prayer is strong. Where there needs to be a number of chalices and ciboria on the altar, they should be arranged in such a way that there is space around a single chalice and paten centrally so that the simple focus is maintained.

The long tradition of mixing a little water with the wine is almost certainly utilitarian in origin. Justin Martyr implies that it was to prevent any possible suggestion of drunkenness at the Eucharist. People identify it with John's account of the blood and water flowing from the side of the lifeless body of Christ. It also provides a link at every Eucharist with the water of baptism. The water first brought us into that company where we now share the bread and wine.

Once the bread and wine are ready upon the altar, Section 33 permits the Roman offertory prayers. *Lent, Holy Week, Easter* provides a modified version that raises no doctrinal problem:

> Blessed are you, Lord, God of the universe,
> you bring forth bread from the earth.
> **Blessed be God for ever**.
>
> Blessed are you, Lord, God of the universe,
> you create the fruit of the vine.
> **Blessed by God for ever**.

Whichever text is preferred, it is worth noting that, in the Roman rite, the prayers would not be spoken out loud when the Eucharist was sung. If there were a hymn of chant sung at this point, the whole table-laying would be done in silence during it.

Section 34 makes provision for the collection and presentation of money. There is sense in the practice of collecting the gifts of money as people enter the church, but if they are to be collected during the liturgy, any who see significance in offering gifts will want it to happen at this point in the service, where it is associated with the bread and wine. What is unfortunate is if the bringing of bread and wine to the table is delayed until the collection is complete, and thus the hymn reaches its end and the preparation is only half done. The connection does not have to be so tight that the money has to arrive at the same moment. The words provided here from 1 Chronicles 29 are, like the earlier Roman prayers, optional. Despite the way they are frequently used, they are clearly intended to refer to the presentation of the collection, not the bread and wine. Especially when there is a hymn, the argument for their omission is strong.

Section 35 is unambiguous: 'At the preparation of the gifts A HYMN may be sung.' This is the first obvious opportunity for a hymn since before the Gospel, and the first since the gathering song for a hymn of some length and substance. The hymn has several functions to perform. It covers the actions involved in preparing the altar and taking and presenting the collection. It moves the service on from word to sacrament. It prepares the people for the praying of the Eucharistic Prayer. If it does its task well, when it comes to an end, everyone will be ready to take off into the dialogue that launches the prayer. But if it has been too short, or very much too long, or simply hasn't encapsulated the mood, the Eucharistic Prayer has to struggle from a bad start. In the end, the choice of hymn is just as crucial as all the other apparently more weighty considerations.

In most churches, some streamlining of the Preparation of the Gifts would benefit the liturgy. It needs to move in a business-like and unwordy way through the preliminaries of preparation, maintaining the dynamic of the service, so that at the beginning of the Eucharistic Prayer hearts may indeed be lifted up to the Lord.

15

GIVING THANKS

A single prayer

Gathered around the altar table, with bread and wine as
their focus, the president and people now pray the
Eucharistic Prayer, one of the high points of the service,
a sustained outpouring of praise, that identifies with
Jesus in the second of his four actions at the Supper, but
develops beyond this into thanksgiving for the mighty
acts of God in a way he could not have done, recalls that
Supper and the words during it, calls down the Holy
Spirit upon the gifts and upon the people, and offers the
duty and service of Christian hearts.

It is a single prayer from opening dialogue to
concluding doxology. It needs different shades and
moods if it is indeed to be a sustained outpouring of
praise, but it remains a unity. Rite A is at pains to
emphasize this, in, for instance, Note 3 which insists:

> The Eucharistic Prayer is a single prayer, the unity of
> which may be obscured by changes of posture in the
> course of it.

This insistence is to counter a tendency to attach greater
weight to some parts of the prayer than to others, and to
look for a moment of consecration. Where the whole
prayer is said fairly speedily and in a matter-of-fact
tone, except for two paragraphs, the account of the
Supper, and if at that moment the president slows down
his speech, takes bread and then cup into his hands and
raises them high, and if at that moment there is the
ringing of bells, it is difficult to avoid the sense that this
is the moment that really counts, and all that comes
before and after is secondary.

Where, as in the Prayer Book rite, the first part of the prayer – Dialogue, Preface and *Sanctus* – is separated from the second part by an intrusion (the Prayer of Humble Access) and only after that does the rubric direct that the priest shall say the Prayer of Consecration, something of the same impression is given.

There is a human need to identify a moment. The whole eucharistic rite is in one sense about focusing the presence of Christ. He is present in the entire celebration. There are those who do not want to say more than that. But Christians have usually wanted to say more. It is in the Eucharistic Prayer that bread and wine are sanctified to be the Body and Blood of Christ. Thus we may see Christ's coming focused in that prayer and his presence in that bread and wine. People may express it, and indeed believe it, in a variety of ways, but to focus to that degree seems right. It is there that the rite tries to hold the line, and it is probably a psychological and devotional need, more than a theological one, that wants to focus still further on particular words or actions. There is no agreement in the Church about whether this is natural and good, or to be resisted as too precise, almost consecration by formula.

Rite A in its rubrics seeks to hold to this wider view that it is through the whole eucharistic action, of which the offering of the whole prayer is the climax, that the bread and wine are set aside to be the Body and Blood of Christ. Those who superimpose on to it the rituals of earlier rites, or those of the Roman rite, are trying to reconcile two differing approaches, and so are not always successful.

The instruction about posture has been mentioned already. The view taken in Rite A is that a change from standing to kneeling after the *Sanctus* (as in the Roman rite) breaks the unity of the prayer and wrongly signals a move to a more significant stage of the prayer.

Similarly the traditional gesture of the president, the 'manual acts' as they have sometimes been called, are discouraged. Whereas, in the Prayer Book rite, taking and breaking were so bound up with giving thanks that manual acts were ordered as part of the Eucharistic Prayer, Rite A has moved 'the taking' into a separate silent gesture before the prayer begins, and 'the breaking' into a stage of its own after the prayer, leaving only 'giving thanks', which has no obvious 'action', and assumes no change of gesture during the prayer itself. Note 16 permits the traditional gestures, but gives them no encouragement, and indeed if the 'taking' rubric is followed at Section 36, further action at the words of institution creates a double taking.

But there are difficulties with this purist view. For some, as indicated above, they are theological. For others, they are much more to do with the drama of the prayer. If it to be a sustained outpouring of praise, it needs to have built within it the variety and the contrasts that make it lively and enable it to command attention. It can be made to feel very long, and demand endurance rather than engender joy.

How does it 'work' as a prayer? It does so partly through its dialogue character. It is long, and it carries a lot of doctrine turned into praise, but it maintains its momentum through the exchanges between president and people, often with the help of music. The opening dialogue establishes this character right at the beginning, and it is carried on through the presidential texts that are punctuated by congregational response in *Sanctus*, *Benedictus*, Acclamations and Amen. The president's own words need to carry the momentum forward and elicit from the people the kind of committed response that also encourages him as the prayer moves forward. It is when this relationship between president and people is lively that the prayer can become a sustained outpouring of praise.

But it can be helped also by the very things of which the Rite A rubrics are suspicious. For they encourage 'sameness' throughout the prayer, where variety will give the prayer its spice. Although he needs to guard against overfilling every phrase with maximùm meaning, the president needs to be sensitive to the fact that different sorts of words require different tones of voice. 'Therefore with angels and archangels . . .' requires quite a different tone from the narrative material that follows soon after in the account of the Supper.

But the variety goes beyond the tone of voice. If the visual counts for anything, and eyes are focused on bread, wine and altar, a motionless president will not convey the dynamism of the prayer. There need to be gestures. They do not need to signal moments of consecration, but they do need, by use of eye and hand, to signify the offering of prayer to heaven and the sense of the Spirit hovering over the celebration. To speak of the Eucharist as a drama, and then to be suspicious of the dramatic at this high point, is confused.

The people and the prayer

The people are helped to offer the prayer by the sensitivity of the president. But their role needs to be exercised by their own prayerful conviction. It begins with the opening Dialogue. Here they give the president their assent and encouragement as he begins to lead their prayer. That is the function of that exchange. He proceeds because they have given their assent. This part of the rite should only be *sung* if the entire congregation can join confidently in its part. This is not a moment when people should stand silently by and allow others to speak for them. Nor, of course, is it a text that any president should delegate to another minister with a better singing voice. These words are between the president and the whole congregation, and must remain so.

From the congregation's point of view we need to re-examine Rite A's concern about a change of posture during the prayer. A move from standing to kneeling after the *Sanctus* cannot be ruled out. It need not be an intrusion (providing it is not introduced by a dreadful 'Let us pray' as if all that had gone before were not prayer). For some a change of posture may enable them to relax into a prayer that would otherwise have kept them standing longer than they can comfortably manage. It may mark, not a break in the prayer, but the move from the straightforward praise of the Preface into a stage where so many different sorts of prayer are subtly drawn together. It is still praise and thanksgiving, but it is the kind of praise that is not unnatural on our knees. This is not to say that there *ought* to be a change of posture. There is a lot to be said for standing throughout. But there is no hard-and-fast rule to be applied in all circumstances.

The people's next response is in the Acclamation. *Patterns for Worship* introduces a greater variety of Eucharistic Prayers, and one of their features is a development of responsive and acclamatory texts. In Rite A there is only the text:

> **Christ has died:**
> **Christ is risen:**
> **Christ will come again.**

Lent, Holy Week, Easter introduced also the more ancient:

> **Dying you destroyed our death.**
> **Rising you restored our life.**
> **Lord Jesus, come in glory.**

Not everyone believes that Rite A has either the best text or the right place in the prayer for it, and the Acclamations are optional. But a response by the people during this phase of the prayer is helpful. Note 15 allows the Acclamations to be introduced by the words, 'Let us proclaim the mystery of faith', or similar words, and this follows the Roman rite. There are problems with this formula. First of all it is an extraordinary phrase. What in this context does 'the mystery of faith' mean? There is the second problem that, if these words are spoken by the president, they intrude into the prayer addressed to the Father an invitation addressed to the congregation. This particular difficulty is removed when the words are spoken instead by the deacon, and that is a logical development of the deacon's role, though even then it can sound like an unwarranted intrusion. If the words are to be spoken by the president, at least they need amending to 'Therefore we proclaim the mystery of faith', or 'Therefore we proclaim our hope', both of which are found in the Canadian *Book of Alternative Services*. Despite Roman practice, perhaps the ASB text has it right in seeking to elicit the Acclamation immediately in response to 'Do this in remembrance of me' without any intervening invitation.

From earliest days the conclusion of the Eucharistic Prayer has been recognized to be special. The people need to give their assent at the end, as well as at the beginning. This must mean a firm Amen. Sometimes this is best achieved by the president breaking into song for the final doxology, so that the people may come in with a sung Amen. An alternative is to provide a more substantial response for them, as in the First Eucharistic Prayer ('Blessing and honour and glory . . .'). Care needs to be taken to ensure that the prayer does build to a climax.

Whatever the concern that manual acts in the middle of the prayer will enhance one part at the expense of another, the raising of the elements at the final doxology – the president the bread, the deacon the cup – is a custom of long standing, and does not focus a particular moment, but confirms that the whole prayer has been significant. The gesture, with the people's strong Amen, makes sure that the prayer ends on a high note. Where the ministers are to bow in reverence, this is the moment, when the whole prayer has come to an end.

The choice of Eucharistic Prayer

Rite A provides four Eucharistic Prayers, similar in shape, style and length. Although there is a strong case for variety, it would be better served if the four were more distinct. *Patterns for Worship* has given four more, not as yet authorized, and these go some way to meet the call for variety, greater congregational response, more possibility of brevity, and for a more visual imagery.

Chapter 6 has already discussed the need to retain a sense of common prayer in the Church of England, and Chapter 7 suggests how the choice of Eucharistic Prayer can help create the mood and character of a particular season. The present legal provision presents a church community with real difficulties at a Eucharist where children predominate. If the use of the Roman Eucharistic Prayers for children is to be discouraged, prayers along the lines of those in *Patterns for Worship* need to be authorized without delay.

Meanwhile the use of Prayer 2, taking advantage of the permission to omit most of the long Preface and to insert a short seasonal one, is the best legal option. If this can be done with Prayer 2, it must also be possible without loss to the theology when using Prayer 1, for the preface material in the two prayers is identical.

The Preface

Rite A has gone far beyond previous services in providing a collection of prefaces that reflect the seasons, and *The Promise of His Glory* and *Enriching the Christian Year* extend this provision further. But there is a case for an unchanging proper preface throughout a season so that it can be deeply assimilated.

In a prayer that cannot admit much spontaneity if it is to be a source of unity at a key moment in liturgy, it would be good, nonetheless, if churches, and eucharistic presidents in particular, developed the art of composing a preface that enabled special moments of thanksgiving in the community to be caught up in the Eucharistic Prayer. This is where such thanksgiving belongs more than in the Prayers of Intercession, and future revision ought to allow freedom for a proper preface locally devised.

16

BREAKING BREAD

The Lord's Prayer

It is natural that the Lord's Prayer finds a place in the eucharistic rite. A case can be made for putting it in one of several different places, and indeed it is found at a variety of points in different rites. Rite A follows the majority in placing it as the first prayer of the pre-communion devotions. The heading 'The Communion' has moved the rite on from thanksgiving to communion. The Lord's Prayer, with its 'Give us this day our daily bread . . .', which acquires a special meaning in this eucharistic context, presses on to the reception of the bread and wine. The petitions relating to forgiveness also make links with the Breaking of Bread and the *Agnus Dei* which follow immediately.

The translation of the Lord's Prayer remains a matter of dispute. There has been a logic in trying to commend to the Church a modernized translation of the Lord's Prayer, in keeping with the contemporary English of the rite. But, logical or not, it has not been accepted in England outside the narrow confines of the Church of England, and even here only in some places and often only with the text in front of people. Other denominations, by far the majority of schools, and a significant minority of churches using Rite A, have stayed with 'Our Father, who art in heaven . . .' It may be that we should accept that England is not ready for a new version, and gracefully come into line.

Patterns for Worship provides some alternative introductions to the Lord's Prayer. Among introductions that are suitable for the Eucharist are:

Let us now pray to the Father in the words our Savious gave us

As we look to the coming of God's kingdom, let us say

Lord, remember us in your kingdom, as following your teaching we say

Jesus taught us to call God our Father, and so in faith and trust we say.

Broken bread

Breaking is the third of the four actions of Jesus. Originally utilitarian, ensuring the bread is broken for all to have a share, it ought now to recover both that utilitarian function, and also to develop more clearly the symbolic meaning that has long been attached to it.

The symbolic goes deeper than the sense of sharing, important as that may be, and is about brokenness itself. The bread that Christ gives in the Eucharist is never just his body, but always his broken body. Something about the scandal of the brokenness of the Church is present, linked with the sense of the Body of Christ broken upon the cross. For that reason alone it is so much better that people receive into their hands bread that is broken, ragged and torn, simply because it is the broken body that redeems, and because the vocation to follow Christ is in part about accepting brokenness. The neat rounded host says nothing of that.

Nor does it say anything about the sharing. It is essentially an individual and private meal for one. Anglicans have long poured scorn on individual cups for communion in the Free Church tradition, a poor substitute for the common cup, and yet have been quite happy to ignore the common loaf. Fortunately there is widespread change; perhaps not for much longer will the individual host survive.

Churches will differ in their solution. Some will go for a genuine loaf, broken apart at this' point in the service.

Others will opt for many of the new sorts of unleavened wafer or biscuit bread, in a variety of sizes, that can be broken for sharing. At very least people may opt for the use of nothing but the larger hosts that can be broken into four, six or eight. Here, even if there is not quite one bread, at least there is breaking.

This is the point in the service where it happens. The oddest thing is where there is a genuine loaf, but it has been cut up before the service, or where there is at this point a purely symbolic breaking, and the ministers then break the bread later as they distribute – confusing two distinct actions, breaking and giving.

The function of the anthem, *Agnus Dei*, 'Lamb of God', which makes so hauntingly the connection between the breaking of the bread and the cross, is to provide a song that can be sung while the breaking is done. Although it is the president who says the words as he breaks the bread into two, the breaking may then continue with as many ministers involved as necessary. If there is a large number to receive communion, there will be several ministers to distribute the bread and wine, and they may join the president and the deacon in breaking the bread while the singing continues. Even at a very large celebration, there is no real excuse for individualized or pre-broken hosts.

The possibility of attaching the Peace to the Breaking of Bread has been discussed in Chapter 13.

The rubrics make both the words and the action of the fraction presidential. It is obviously right that the president breaks, though others might assist him. It is difficult to see why the deacon might not say the words that accompany the breaking, especially when, like the Rite A text, they are addressed to the people.

Rite A provides only one text for the bread-breaking, but all the supplementary books introduce a variety, seasonal in tone, and several include the ancient text based on the *Didache*:

Creator of all, we have gathered many grains
and made them into this one bread.
**We look for your Church to be gathered
from the ends of the earth into the kingdom.**

Communion for the sick

When the bread is broken, it may include provision for
the communion of the sick and housebound. Sometimes,
where there is a theology of 'extended distribution',
authorized ministers, ordained or lay, will go straight
from the service, either after the distribution or after the
Dismissal, to take the sacrament to them. But in other
communities, the communion will be taken to them
during the week. When this is the case, bread and wine
should be set aside for this purpose at the principal
Eucharist of the week, and at this point, during the
Breaking and the *Agnus Dei*, taken by the deacon or
another minister and placed in the aumbry, any that
remains from the previous week being brought out to be
consumed with what remains over at this celebration.
By 'reserving' at this main Eucharist, and by placing of
the bread and wine in the aumbry at this point, the
unity of the housebound communicant with the rest of
the Body of Christ is affirmed.

17

FEEDING ON CHRIST

Making communion

The fourth of the actions of Jesus is the giving of the bread and wine. In the accounts of the Last Supper he gives to those at table with him. In other stories of eucharistic character, the feeding of multitudes, he gives to the disciples so that they may distribute.

What is going on in this fourth action? People describe it in a variety of ways. People entitle the whole service 'Holy Communion', but they also refer at this point to 'taking communion', 'making communion' and 'receiving communion'. In the past this section of the service was often simply called 'The Communion'. Rite A insists on holding to the biblical word and speaks of 'The Giving of the Bread and Cup', though it also refers to what is going on as 'the distribution'. Yet today one of the most popular phrases is 'sharing communion', though that appears nowhere in the rites. There is truth in all these terms, and the appeal of 'sharing' is obvious in an age that has wanted to regain the sense of the corporate in the Eucharist. For people did indeed speak, perhaps some still do, not simply of 'making communion' but of 'making *my* communion', an excessively individualistic description that ignored all those around who shared in the celebration and in the receiving around the altar. It has been a natural and proper corrective to put an emphasis on the truth that we come to God together, that we relate to one another as we worship, that only being the Body can we receive the Body, and that our communion is with each other as well as with our Lord.

Yet I believe we must now guard against the opposite danger that we shall see the distribution of the bread and wine almost entirely in terms of a fellowship meal in which we share, blessed by God certainly, but where the giving is very much of ourselves to one another. This is illustrated by the way some people minister to one another in distributing the sacrament, holding the experience at the level of communication between two people.

But the giving of the bread and the cup is a solemn moment of encounter with Christ. However we understand it precisely, we are sharing principally with *him*, renewing our participation in his death and resurrection, and receiving his life into our life. Because that is what is going on fundamentally, I chose to call this chapter 'Feeding on Christ', picking up on the phrase in the invitation to communion ('Feed on him in your hearts'), not because I want to deny all the other things that are going on, but because I fear lest we lose sight of a deep mystery.

I fear lest we become Christians who trip too happily to the altar for the family meal. We should not come trusting in our own righteousness, and we are not worthy so much as to gather up the crumbs. Yes, at another level we have been *counted* worthy to stand in God's presence and serve him. But the approach should be filled with wonder, with longing, and with a desire for nothing less than communion with the living God. Somehow, without losing all the welcome contemporary insights that had become obscured, we need to recover something of that truth. Together we come to have communion with our Saviour, and to feed on Christ in our hearts.

The invitation

With the breaking of the bread complete, the president invites the congregation to draw near to receive. The intention is that this invitation should precede any reception of the elements, even by the ministers. Their receiving of communion is not of a different order from other people's. It certainly should not happen during *Agnus Dei*, which is an anthem for the breaking, not the giving.

The normative text for inviting the people to receive begins with the words 'Draw near', and that is meant to be a literal invitation, so that, even if the ministers in the sanctuary are the first to receive, they do so with others coming up and gathering around them, witnessing to the fact that it is one communion in which all share.

The invitation 'Draw near with faith' is required to be said on Sundays and Holy Days, whether or not additional words are used. This is because it contains the classic Anglican description of what happens in receiving communion. The communicants receive the Body of Christ given for them and his Blood shed for them. They eat and drink in remembrance of him. They feed on him in their hearts by faith with thanksgiving. In the Prayer Book rite, that is said to every communicant. In this rite, where a much briefer formula is permitted in addressing each communicant, that classic text of the Anglican position is enshrined in this mandatory invitation.

But there are additional forms of invitation. The Rite A appendix provides three, one for the period from Easter Day to Pentecost, reinforcing the picture of the Eucharist as a paschal meal, the others for more general use. 'Jesus is the Lamb of God' takes up the *Agnus Dei* theme in a text adapted from the Roman rite. Rome has '*This* is the Lamb of God', but Rite A '*Jesus* is the Lamb of God'. It allows for wider theological interpretation.

The Promise of His Glory has introduced two more forms. The first originates with All Saints' Day and is suitable for the festival of any saint:

I heard the voice of a great multitude crying, Alleluia!
The Lord our God has entered into his kingdom.
**Blessed are those who are called to the supper of
the Lamb.**

The other is given for Christmas:

> Christ is the bread which has come down from
>   heaven.
> **Lord, give us this bread for ever**.

The distribution

Rite A does not specify who shall receive first. It contents
itself with: 'The president and people receive the
communion'. This is in contrast to the Prayer Book
where the priest is to receive before anyone else. Some of
those who framed the new rite were anxious to commend
the practice of the ministers communicating last. On
many occasions it would make for a swifter move into
the general distribution, so that the momentum of the
rite is not lost at that point. It also might seem to be
good manners; serving yourself last.

There is, however, another view, that because the
president and the ministers are not the hosts of the rite –
only Christ is the host – that is a false argument, and
they need to receive the sacrament first to be made
worthy to share it with others. Both viewpoints have
some sense to them. Certainly, when people have always
been accustomed to seeing the ministers receive first
and to wait their turn, to set aside that tradition at least
makes them think about the nature of the Church.

Where the ministers do receive first, there is no need
for all in the sanctuary to receive in some sort of
hierarchical order. All, ministers and servers, gather
around the table, the circle open so as to admit
symbolically the rest of the congregation to it, and share
first the bread and then the cup, perhaps with the words
being spoken once only and the elements passed in
silence. So often the Eucharist seems to come to a
grinding halt, at what should be a moment of expectation
for the people, simply because the distribution within
the sanctuary is so laborious.

In Chapter 2 there was some discussion about who

may distribute the communion. There is nothing priestly about it. The president will very likely want to share in the distribution. When he is the parish priest it is an important moment for him pastorally, moving along the line of communicants, knowing so many of the people by name. Nevertheless, sometimes when there are sufficient ministers, there is some point in his not doing so, especially at a great service that demands much of him. This is one of his opportunities to withdraw into prayer and so to uphold the celebration in a different way.

The ideal is that all the communicants may draw near to the altar of the celebration and receive around or in front of it, whether kneeling or standing (see Chapter 5). There are occasions when numbers dictate the use of other altars or 'stations' around the building, for it is important that the distribution should not take so long that the service loses its impetus. When it does, it hardly ever recovers it. But, even with side altars and stations, it is desirable that everyone should move in the direction of the central focus. When people walk away from the altar to receive, something is lost. This is not always achievable, but everything starts from the desirability of all being drawn together towards the altar of the celebration.

Some of those who come forward are not communicants. We owe it to people to make clear in our churches, whether on notice boards or service sheets, sometimes by a word from the president or deacon in the service itself, who is welcome to receive communion, and how others, whatever their age, are invited to come forward to receive a blessing. It is important that no one feels second class or unwelcome or just uncertain about where they stand.

During the distribution, the rubric (Section 47) permits hymns and anthems, and again this must be taken broadly to include chants and choruses. But they need to be suitable to this moment in the rite. People are drawing near to make their communion, to feed on

Christ. The music must enhance that spirit of approach, not challenge it or drown it. Silence between music is also a blessing. It may of course be spoilt by idle chatter unless people have been taught to use this time well.

18

GOING OUT

After Communion

The final part of the service, from distribution to Dismissal, has two functions. It needs to enable people to assimilate the reception of the sacrament, in a sense to remain 'in communion'. But it needs after that, not just to let them go, but to send them out, equipped and motivated, for living the Christian gospel in daily life. The difficulty is in doing both, and there can be a tension between these aims.

It found its most acute expression in the 1960s in the contrast between the ending of the service in the Prayer Book rite and in the first new rite, Holy Communion Series 2. The Prayer Book has a long, extended and glorious 'After Communion' section. Its theology has given it a shape where the community only takes off into sheer praise after receiving communion, and so Lord's Prayer, fine prayers of 'thanksgiving' and 'oblation', and the *Gloria* all belong to this part of the service. The soul is fed not only by the reception of communion, but by this rich material that holds the communicant in communion. But there is not much sense of being sent out, no hint of mission, no dismissal. In the way that the rite has often been celebrated, after the Blessing, if there were music, it would be quiet and meditative, not wanting to intrude.

But Holy Communion Series 2, because it had restored the sense of praise and thanksgiving right through the service, and especially in the Eucharistic Prayer, insisted on a quite different ending. A short and rather ungracious prayer, without a hint of 'thank you' but with an emphasis on sending out, was followed by a dismissal. There was a blessing, but it was optional, and the purists discouraged it. What further blessing was needed after the grace of communion? The post-communion shape was turned on its head. Once communion had been received, it was all 'get up and go'.

Theoretically there was much to commend this emphasis. Devotionally it was a shock to those brought up on the Prayer Book ending. Liturgically time revealed that it was unsatisfactory. People needed time and space before being propelled out.

The 'After Communion' section in Rite A is something of a compromise between these two endings, but this is right, for, at most celebrations, there needs to be both a time to stay and reflect, and also a time to be sent out.

Before looking at how this can be developed through the final sections of the service, we need to look at two practicalities.

The first is the instruction in section 49 that 'any consecrated bread and wine which is not required for purposes of communion is consumed at the end of the distribution or after the service'. The 'ablutions' do not have any symbolic significance. Obviously there is a doctrinal implication in the Church of England's insistence that what remains is consumed, rather than re-used or thrown away, and a rubric insisting on this tries to ensure that this is done, and done immediately and decently. But it is still essentially a practical thing, to be done quietly and unobtrusively. In particular the practice of consuming what remains and cleansing the vessels at the altar is unfortunate at a celebration facing the people. It is unseemly to consume the left-overs and do the washing up in full view of the guests.

What remains at the end of the distribution should not be returned to the altar, but taken to the credence table, or even to the vestry or a side chapel, and there consumed and the vessels cleansed with as little fuss as possible, if possible by the deacon or another minister, so that the president may not be encumbered with this task. Where it can be done discreetly and speedily, it may follow the distribution immediately, or be done, when there is one, during the final hymn. Where, at a great service, the task is greater, it should wait until immediately after the service has ended. It should not delay the service, and any silence after communion should not appear to be simply to allow time for washing up.

There is the question also of where the 'After Communion' part of the service is to be focused. It need not be at the altar, though often this will seem the most convenient place. It may be from the president's chair. It may be back where the Ministry of the Word was celebrated. This may be right if the altar and sanctuary are not well-placed and have been used only when the altar needed to be the focus.

Silence and prayer

Of all the periods of prayer in the Eucharist, the one that follows the distribution is the one with most potential for development. It is a matter of building on the atmosphere of prayer and communion that has reached its climax as people have come to receive. Returning to their places, and perhaps sitting, rather than kneeling, they can be encouraged to be still, to reflect and to pray, in other words to 'remain in communion'. When the distribution is over, the president and other ministers, having placed what remains of the bread and wine on a table, also sit and join in this period of silence, the whole community still.

People will differ on whether this silence needs the stimulus of a sentence of Scripture or chant or other song, or whether the communion itself provides sufficient way in. Rite A allows for a sentence of Scripture, and provides one for each day, picking up on the seasonal and thematic emphasis. This is all that is left of an older tradition of psalmody during the distribution. When the sentence is sung during the distribution it is not an intrusion. If it is spoken by the president before he sits down, it could be, if the silence has already been established. In the Roman rite the president sometimes speaks it immediately before the distribution, anticipating its proper place, and this too tends to be an intrusion at the moment of reception. The function of the sentence is to stimulate the prayerfulness of the silence, and it should be used only if it does that rather than interrupt.

The natural conclusion of this time of prayer is a collect, parallel to the Collect that drew to an end the time of prayer at the beginning of the rite, though the collect at this later point will need to carry some sense of thanksgiving for what has been received and of the impetus to go out to serve.

The Rite A rubric at Section 51 allows for any suitable prayer, but then two are provided, one a presidential text, the other a congregational one. This second prayer (Section 53) is well-established and is a development of the Series 2 'send us out' prayer. Unlike the Series 2 version (still found in the Rite A Appendix, but with the language modernized), there is an element of thankfulness, though it is restrained, since thanksgiving after communion should not detract from the primary thanksgiving of the Eucharistic Prayer.

Where there is a desire to have alternative congregational prayers after communion, a number of those in *Patterns for Worship* are written in a style suited to being said together.

But there is also a case for a presidential concluding collect, slightly different in style, and bringing the service back at this point to its seasonal character. The Rite A prayer at Section 52 is a fine composition, though it has proved more effective with occasional, rather than daily, use, for it is almost too rich in imagery. (Unlike most presidential prayers it also works well as a congregational text, and may sometimes be substituted for 'Almighty God, we thank you . . .' after a presidential collect.) The new supplementary books have all provided post-communion prayers for each festival and season, and Charles

MacDonnell's compilation, *After Communion* (Mowbray 1985), also provides one for every day.

Although theoretically one prayer ought to suffice, whether presidential and variable, or congregational and standard, experience suggests that, at this point in the rite, the two prayers, one after the other, are helpful. The president's variable text sums up the collective silence, the congregation's prayer begins the process of sending out.

A final song

At the main Eucharist, at some stage in this concluding part of the rite, there will be a final hymn or song. Quite what its character needs to be will depend a little on where it is placed in the development of this final section. It may, like a seasonal prayer, bring back at the end the particular theme or emphasis of that day's celebration. It may strike a note of thanksgiving, especially at the end of a season or at the conclusion of a project, though, like the prayer after communion, it will not want to detract from the focus on thanksgiving in the Eucharistic Prayer earlier in the rite. Very often it is the hymn, more than anything else, that can move the mood of the service on into the final phase of 'sending out'. The kind of hymn that reminds people of their vocation, of the Church's mission, of Christianity lived out in daily life, helps turn their minds towards the task before them.

When is this hymn to be sung? Rite A gives as its preferred place the point after the scripture sentence that follows the distribution. If the sentence had led into silence, the hymn would emerge from that. That can work well. People sit quietly at prayer and then stand to sing, the hymn acting rather like a collect to draw their prayer together. Then the prayers follow the hymn. The people will be standing for the prayer, and that will give it a particular character, and blessing and dismissal will follow.

Alternatively, the hymn might follow the prayer. That

is also a natural sequence. Silence leads into prayer. The prayer introduces the 'sending out' theme, and people stand, the first move towards going out, and sing a hymn that strengthens their resolve. Then comes the Dismissal, and they are ready to go.

In some settings, there may be a need to sing the hymn after the Blessing to cover the withdrawal of the ministers, but this is not ideal (see following section). What is worse is a hymn after the Dismissal itself, rendering meaningless the invitation to the people to 'go in peace'.

The dismissal

To this section belong the Blessing, the final words of dismissal themselves, and, at a practical level, the dispersal of the community. For some there is also within this section, the giving of Notices. We have already noted that this might precede the service (given out by a minister other than the president) or come within the service before the Prayers of Intercession. If they are to be kept for this last stage of the liturgy, so that they become part of the sending out, they should precede, not follow, the Dismissal.

The Blessing is an optional element in the rite. Some believe that the communion constitutes the ultimate blessing, after which presidential words are superfluous. Others think that a blessing needs to mark a special occasion, rather than form part of the liturgy week in week out. But the Blessing survives in most communities. There is in many people an ingrained sense of its appropriateness at the end of a service. There is also nowadays, at least at the main Sunday liturgy, a strong likelihood of non-communicants being present, not all of whom will have come to the altar to be blessed.

Where there is a blessing, Rite A provides in its main text the treasured Anglican blessing form that Cranmer put into his first rite in 1549. Other seasonal blessings appear in the Appendix, and *Patterns for Worship, The*

Promise of His Glory and *Enriching the Christian Year* provide more. These include 'Solemn Blessings', each with three clauses prior to the usual trinitarian formula of the final clause. In most of these the whole shape of the prayer is also trinitarian, with each of the first three clauses referring to one person of the Trinity. These solemn blessings are intended to mark days of special significance. They should be used sparingly if they are to retain that quality of being special.

The people are often sent out with the sign of the cross, made over them by the president as he gives the Blessing. They have celebrated Christ's death upon the cross and his resurrection, and now they are going out, marked with the cross, to tell the good news of his salvation from day to day. So it is right and proper that they should be dismissed with this sign, made over them strongly and boldly.

All that remains is for them to be told to go. Although at Section 55 Rite A assigns this text to the president, it is not listed in the earlier note as his prerogative, and by tradition it is the deacon who says or sings the Dismissal. Rite A provides two forms, and encourages a double Alleluia on each part throughout the fifty days from Easter Day to Pentecost.

There remains only the question of how 'the ministers and people depart'. Whereas there is important symbolism in the movement of the ministers through the congregation at the beginning of the liturgy, there is no equivalent significance in their departure. A procession to the altar is a symbolic pilgrimage; a 'recession' (with its 'recessional hymn') is a strange Anglican invention. Moving away from the altar singing does not have the point that moving towards it singing holds.

Quite the contrary. What, if anything, is symbolized at the end of the rite is that the assembly is dismissed and begins to disperse (even if only to post-service coffee). The ministers are part of that dispersal, and the choir has also been dismissed. The ideal therefore is that, after the Blessing and Dismissal, the ministers and the choir, where it is robed, move in order, but with minimum fuss and ceremony, out of the church, and the other members of the congregation begin to do so too.

When the ministers reach the vestry there is nothing more liturgically to be said. The assembly has been dismissed already. It does not need another dismissal, least of all one spoken in such a way that the people still in the church are intended to overhear it as a final extra ending. Music that is played at this stage also needs to give the same message: 'The Eucharist is ended. Go in peace.'

Part IV

19

CELEBRATING WITHIN WIDE LIMITS

The need for variety and freedom

Not everybody recognizes the need for new freedom in the ordering of liturgy. It is not just that some see in it a threat to things they hold dear, or even to the identity of the Church of England, but that they cannot perceive any need to make liturgy less constricting.

It is not, of course, sufficient answer to assert that canon law, as at present defined, is frequently flouted. Law-breaking is not of itself justification for new law-making, though sometimes it is the breaking of the law that reveals it as unnecessarily constricting law. There are occasions when the Eucharist needs to be set free.

Some of them have been identified in the course of this book. Law-abiding Anglicans cannot at present substitute Prayer Book texts, other than sung ones, within the modern language rite. They cannot use the *Kyrie* as a confession or a seasonal text instead of the set one at the Breaking of the Bread. They cannot dispense with the set Sunday readings in order to follow a different carefully planned course even on the neutral Sundays before Lent and after Pentecost. They cannot employ a Eucharistic Prayer with wider use of responses and acclamations than those in Rite A. None of these are outrageous suggestions that threaten common prayer or doctrine. All of these are freedoms that ought to be available, week by week and Sunday by Sunday in any celebration.

Beyond these simple and mainly uncontroversial new freedoms, there is a need to allow greater flexibility in certain prescribed circumstances. Three sorts of circumstances suggest themselves.

The first is one where a great many of those present are unfamiliar with the Eucharist and with the traditions that churchpeople take for granted. The Eucharist is rich in image and symbol, and its texts have often gone deeply into the souls of those who have lived and worshipped with them a long time. But unless we are to allow the Eucharist to be only for the initiated (as indeed it was early in Christian history, but see Chapter 24 later), we need sometimes to celebrate it with a particular eye to those who are unused to it. Within this category will often be children. Where they form the majority of the congregation (and that can happen even when they are not the majority of the communicants) their needs are paramount.

But it is not only with children that we have to develop this sensitivity to occasion. If the liturgy has the power to convert, and God wants to use the Eucharist as a tool of evangelism, that will sometimes, not always, need to be through a Eucharist that is willing to stand on the periphery of Christian life.

We also need to consider those whose lack of familiarity is not with the Eucharist, but with our English traditions. In our multicultural society, there need to be opportunities for the cross-fertilization of our English experience and other Christian cultures, some of them Anglican in origin, that have come among us.

The second circumstance is when Christian people are gathered to share in a time of experiment outside their usual church experience. It may be a 'Parish Weekend' during which worship, like everything else, will want to explore new styles, and to push the boundaries back, even if only so that people may discover for themselves, and validate, just why the boundaries are normally where they are. It may not usually be the role of the Eucharist to challenge and confront, but in particular settings it needs to be allowed to be very different, so that it can express its vitality along fresh lines, and be a vehicle of new experiences of God.

The third circumstance is in ecumenical settings.

Canon Law allows some additional freedoms in Local Ecumenical Projects (LEPs). But most people do not live in LEPs, yet they sometimes come together with Christians of traditions other than theirs, and desire that their worship shall reflect their different traditions and styles, yet still be eucharistic.

In all these different circumstances, some of which (like a school Eucharist) we may encounter weekly, others of which (like the Parish Weekend or the ecumenical service) may happen only rarely, there is need for freedom and the opportunity for variety beyond not just the letter, but the spirit, of ASB provision.

Setting the boundaries

The reluctance to grant new freedom arises from a well-justified fear that it will accelerate a decline into a new kind of congregationalism in which every church community 'does its own thing', and often its own unliturgical thing. Mention has already been made of the importance in Church of England terms of common prayer (see Chapter 6). Where are the boundaries to be set?

Patterns for Worship identified seven marks of Anglican worship that needed to be safeguarded if people wished 'to stand in any recognizable continuity with historic Anglican tradition'. It did not of course claim that these marks were not present in other churches. The seven were:

A recognizable structure for worship;

An emphasis on reading the word and on using psalms;

Liturigical words repeated by the congregation, some of which, like the Creed, would be known by heart;

Using a collect, the Lord's Prayer, and some responsive forms in prayer;

A recognition of the centrality of the Eucharist;

A concern for form, dignity and economy of words;

A willingness to use forms and prayers which can be used across a broad spectrum of Christian belief.

To those seven, to which I subscribe, I would add three more. I believe Church of England worship has:

An important place for penitence in public worship;

A recognition of the value of the Christian year and its seasons;

An emphasis, especially through creeds and canticles, on praising God for what he has done.

No Christian Church, I suspect, invites its members to say the creeds as often as the Church of England, and, although few follow the Prayer Book's invitation to recite the Creed morning and evening every day, there does permeate Anglican worship a desire for objectivity, and a biblical emphasis that expresses God's praise classically, not so much in saying who he is and giving him glory for that, but in recalling what he has done and giving the glory for that. It stands rather over against the emphasis in some churches today, where 'a time of worship' can glorify God without the kind of historical content to the praise that has been the mark of Church of England worship in the past.

These ten marks need to be present, to some extent or other, in the life of a Church of England parish if it is to be true to its roots, and the law ought to help set the boundaries at these points. When we are speaking of the Eucharist in particular, the marks should surely include the requirement of using a eucharistic prayer authorized in the Church of England? Without a concern for these marks, there is very real danger that people, robbed both of recognizable shape and structure to worship and also of familiar texts, old or quite new, will find that they have no common prayer, and that there is nothing distinctively Anglican in their worship.

When visitors walk into a church that calls itself 'Church of England', they have a right to expect that the worship will be, not exactly what they have at home, but something with sufficient 'family likeness' for them to experience a sense of belonging. They have a right to be aggrieved if what they receive is so diluted that their own tradition is not coming through, or if the rite of another Church is being used. It has been the Anglican instinct from its very beginning to draw into its worship the liturgical treasures of other traditions, wherever they suit its ethos and character. Thus Anglicans can never reject a particular prayer or ritual or hymn simply on the grounds that it is 'Roman Catholic' or 'Free Church'. But they have always assimilated without loss of identity. Therefore they have not authorized the use of the entire Roman Mass or Methodist Sunday Service. Nor should they unless the day comes when they see no distinctive future for Anglicanism.

Alongside new freedoms and a recognition of their limits, there ought to be also a greater sensitivity about when the freedoms should be pressed to the limits. Some freedoms should not normally be exercised in the Sunday liturgy. They belong to informal groups or special occasions. Others do need to find a place in the Sunday provision but perhaps only once a month, at a Eucharist geared more than in other weeks to children or enquirers. Some freedoms may be appropriate on occasions, but not on occasions when people come together from different places to celebrate their common heritage or when people ought to see the Church at its most normal. For one of the crucial things about granting the freedom to depart, for good reason, from the norm, is that the norm needs to be experienced regularly. If the Creed is said only four times a year, a full form of confession only in Lent, and Rite A Eucharistic Prayers are abandoned week by week in favour of Eucharistic Prayers for children, the norm cannot hold its own.

Law and liturgical formation

If the Church of England wishes to proceed down the path that creates more freedom, but also affirms more strongly the need for common prayer and a limit to diversity, it must do so with two changes of heart that have policy implications. Both are initially in the hands of the bishops.

Firstly, having reformed the law relating to the Eucharist, whether in the canons or in the services themselves, and having created wider freedoms and defined their limits, the Church needs to exercise its discipline and to enforce its law. The whole process of synodical and parliamentary legislation to ensure that the liturgy of the Church of England is true to its doctrinal and historical roots is pointless if the law is not widely followed. The Church cannot allow the Roman Mass or a congregational service with no liturgical form to displace the Church's authorized liturgy without authority being brought into disrepute. Every bishop, priest or deacon taking office promises to use only those services that are 'authorised or allowed by canon'. Some of them probably do not even know exactly what that means.

Since most law-breaking is the result not so much of wickedness as of ignorance, even more useful than the enforcement of law will be the resourcing of liturgical formation. Clergy and laity alike need far more help than they are receiving now in understanding the liturgy and celebrating it with lively confidence. Liturgy is almost entirely unresourced in the Church, and much of the beauty and power of worship described in this book will remain pious pipe-dream until the Church and its bishops look to provide this assistance.

The Church will more happily grant greater liberty in worship when it is clear that liturgical principles will be followed and freedom not abused.

20

CELEBRATING WITH BAPTISM

Baptism at the Sunday liturgy

The ASB notes on page 241 that 'Holy Baptism is normally administered by the parish priest in the course of public worship on Sunday', and also that the service 'should normally be used at Holy Communion or Morning and Evening Prayer'.

That of course is not the end of the matter. There are parishes where the number of baptisms would mean several candidates presented for baptism at the main Sunday service week after week, so that baptism could very easily take the service over, and drive the regular congregation away.

There are other parishes where the clergy believe that more harm than good is done to 'fringe' Christians by being put through the Eucharist (or Morning Prayer) when what they have come for is the baptism of a child. Even when the parents and godparents of the candidate are members of the church community, there will always be many relatives and friends who are out of their depth.

That has not been my experience, and I would plead for baptism at Sunday worship, and especially at the Eucharist, for three reasons beyond the simple fact that the canons and service books make it normal practice.

The first is the one most commonly expressed. It can make no sense to welcome a candidate into an absent community. Baptism is not into the local Church. It is not even into the Church of England. It is into the one holy catholic and apostolic Church, but that experience does need rooting in a worshipping community. The Welcome, when expressed only by the child's family, the minister, and maybe a token member of the congregation or two, is a poor thing. When baptism is celebrated more privately, it is a loss to the candidate and family that the church community is missing, and it is a loss to the church community that it is not faced with its responsibility for the child.

For all its logic, I do not believe that this is the most persuasive reason for baptism at the Sunday Eucharist. A stronger reason is that the Church misses a pastoral and evangelistic opportunity of the first order if it does not seize the opportunity to draw people, who by the very nature of the occasion are more than usually open to the Spirit, into the experience of Christian worship. If we have confidence in our liturgy, and if we have planned the service clearly, when we bring them into an atmosphere of Christian worship, it ought to touch their hearts with the good news of Christ. At a private baptism, people, ill-equipped to do so, have to create an atmosphere of worship all of their own out of nothing. In the liturgy it is different.

There is a third reason. An important need in the Church today is to help people to rediscover the significance of their baptism, to stop regarding it primarily as something that happened once upon a time, and to see it instead as a life into which they have been called. In celebrating the sacrament of baptism Christian people are put in mind of their own baptism. Furthermore when they celebrate baptism within the Eucharist they are helped to make the connection between these two sacraments of Christ.

There is the opposite possibility, that when baptism is celebrated too frequently, and dominates the service too often, far from enhancing the status of baptism, it devalues it in the popular mind. A church needs to guard against that danger, but not to use it as an excuse for celebrating baptism in a more private way.

Baptism at the Eucharist can be celebrated in such a way that it does not take over the service, that the whole service does not last too long, that strangers and visitors need not feel lost or excluded. Where this is not the case, it is a failure of our imagination as we plan the service, rather than any fault in the rite we are given as a basis for the celebration.

Baptism need not take over. The sermon need not be about baptism every time, though perhaps it can be drawn in at some point. Baptismal material need not be substituted at every point through the service. The Sunday readings need not be superseded. Not all that the ASB allows to be omitted from the Eucharist need be omitted if the normal flow of the service needs to be retained.

The extent to which baptism should 'take over' the character of the service will depend both on the frequency of baptism in a particular church, and also on the season of the year. There are times when the liturgy makes all the connections – the Baptism of Christ, Easter, Pentecost. There are other times when it will be important that baptismal themes do not take the service over to the exclusion of Christian festivals and seasons that strike a different note. But there is also the neutral part of the year when a richer baptismal emphasis might give shape to the day's celebration. *Enriching the Christian Year* provides a full text of baptismal texts for the Eucharist, and the ASB itself has a wide provision of baptismal lections.

The minister of baptism

The ASB states that the parish priest is the normal minister of baptism, and within the Eucharist there is a natural expectation that the president of the Eucharist will preside over the baptismal liturgy too. In many places this will be very natural, but in some church communities it would mean that some members of the clergy team, and especially deacons, would never baptize. Presuming that the minister who baptized also undertook the development of the pastoral relationship with the family that preceded baptism, the result of a parish policy to baptize normally at the Eucharist could be to restrict this whole area of ministry to the parish priest.

But the tradition recognizes a liturgical ministry for deacons in baptism, and the ASB in its Baptism and Confirmation order permits a delegation of parts of the initiation rite. On this basis, the president and deacon would minister side by side, as at other points in the Eucharist, the president retaining to himself the presidential functions of questioning the sponsors, saying the prayer over the water and introducing the Welcome. He could delegate to the deacon or to another priest, who might have prepared the family for the baptism, the signing with the cross, the 'baptizing' (in the sense of the dipping in water or pouring of water in the name of the Trinity) and the giving of light. Here are distinctive roles for the two ministers that maintain the presidency of the rite, but recognize the pastoral ministry that others may have in relation to the candidate and family.

The font

It is when baptism is celebrated in public worship that the temptation is strongest in some churches to abandon the use of the font, and to baptize instead at a portable or temporary font in the sanctuary. This cannot always be avoided. If there are several candidates, the baptistry area may be simply too small. Even if there is only one candidate, it may be so badly sited that the congregation would not really witness the baptism.

But there is real loss in abandoning the font, and it ought not to be done lightly. There is the loss in moving baptism from its symbolic place at the place of entry. There is loss in not using the one font that is the symbol of the one baptism. There is the loss that the candidates cannot in future years come back to see and maybe to pray at the font of their baptism. There is the loss when only small quantities of water are used because the temporary font is not much more than a bowl. All in all, it is desirable that at least the 'water rite' be at the font, with a procession to it, and the congregation turning to face it. If its position is a poor one, there is a good case for the Decision and the Signing with the Cross before baptism, and the Giving of Light and the Welcome after baptism being staged where they can be better seen and heard.

Dovetailing rites

ASB page 250 sets out how the Baptism of Children is to be integrated into the Eucharistic rite. It lays down that the Eucharist shall proceed as usual until the sermon. After the sermon, the Creed, Intercession and Prayers of Penitence (unless they have already been used at the Preparation) are omitted and replaced by the Baptism (omitting superfluous readings and prayers). After the Welcome, the Eucharist continues with the Peace. On this basis, what is omitted would probably have taken longer than what replaces it, so there is no danger of the rite being lengthened.

But it is worth examining the omissions that this schedule envisages. The first omission is the Nicene Creed. This is right. The Eucharist is sustainable without it, and, after the sponsors' profession of faith, there is a brief trinitarian affirmation by the whole congregation immediately before the baptism. What needs to be resisted is the turning of every baptism into a renewal of the congregation's baptismal vows. The renewal of vows is a solemn undertaking that should be used rarely and after preparation, probably only at the Feast of the Baptism of Christ and at Easter. Renewal at the drop of a hat devalues.

The second proposed omission is the Intercession Prayer, and this involves real loss, especially if baptism is celebrated at the Eucharist often. If time will allow, there is good argument for restoring intercession, however brief, after the baptism, with a mention of the newly baptized when praying for the Church. *Enriching the Christian Year* gives two forms of intercession with a baptismal flavour. One of them is an abbreviation of the ASB Litany, which could be sung as the procession moves to or from the font. An alternative, time-saving, approach is advocated in Eucharistic Prayer B of *Patterns for Worship*, where brief intercession is drawn into the Eucharistic Prayer when there has been a baptism. The restoration of intercession into the Eucharistic Prayer is, in any case, much to be welcomed.

The third omission is the Penitence, at least in churches where this customarily comes at the later point. Here there is a strong argument, whatever the normal custom, for inserting it at the Preparation. To omit penitence altogether is not easily justified. But, particularly because the service must not grow too long, this is an obvious occasion for the use of the penitential *Kyrie*, rather than a fuller form.

One possible addition from the Baptism rite is the prayer for the candidate's family (ASB page 249 Section 60). Though the rubrics allow its omission, it is a pity to do so, and it may be said at the font after the Welcome. Its rather impersonal tone is improved no end by being turned into a blessing, with the names of the members of the family. The president should use the prayer more than once if there is more than one candidate, rather than try to combine them all into one omnibus blessing. In its blessing form it reads,

> May the heavenly Father bless you, N (and N)
> in your care of N (and NN).
> May he give you the spirit of wisdom and love,
> that your home may reflect the joy of his eternal
>   kingdom.

Whether a blessing of the family has been introduced or not, and whether Intercession Prayers have been restored or not, the rite returns to the usual eucharistic order with the Peace, which has a particular significance at baptism where it seals the sacrament and becomes a deeper sign of welcome to the candidate than the ASB's rather laboured 'We welcome you . . . .' Permission to omit that Welcome and the use of the Peace to express the welcome would be an improvement to the rite.

On that basis, there is a case for the Prayers of Intercession, if there are some, coming from the font, so that the liturgy is still focused there for the Peace. The president will probably choose to use the standard Rite A introduction to the Peace. It strikes the right note on this occasion:

> We are the Body of Christ. In the one Spirit we were all baptized into one body . . .

If the Peace is the expression of welcome, the president will greet the newly baptized. When this is a baby, the appropriate gesture must surely be a kiss?

The Church's pastoral and theological confusion is demonstrated here. The president affirms that we are made members of the Body of Christ by baptism. But the Eucharist proceeds and the newly baptized member of the Body is not admitted to communion. It is to the question of children at the Eucharist that we now turn.

21

CELEBRATING WITH CHILDREN

Basic affirmations

The Church has a lot of guilt about its children, and indeed its lack of them. Commissions sit, reports are written, helpful courses are devised. There are model parishes that seem to get their children's work right, but most places struggle. It isn't always that churchpeople have a negative view that children are, in the common sense of the phrase, 'in the way'. They are affirmative of the place of children in church life and worship. But somehow they haven't found a formula that integrates all ages. There seem to me to be some helpful principles from which to begin, but I struggle with their application as much as anyone else.

The first principle is that children belong at the celebration. They are not in church on sufferance. They do not come in from where they really belong to share a part of it, or go out after a token gesture to where they really ought to be. They are not in training as the Church of tomorrow. They belong, simply by virtue of their baptism, to the Church of today. That has to be the starting-point.

The second is that they belong at the altar, sharing the sacrament. Here we immediately run into a problem, for the Church of England seems unable to grapple with this issue with a determination to bring its pastoral practice into line with its beliefs. If the Church is not going to admit children to communion, it needs to rethink the whole strategy of its worship away from the Family Eucharist concept. It is both unjust and ill-advised to place emphasis on the community gathered around the

Lord's table, and then deny the family meal to a significant part of the membership. Children should either be communicants or they should not be there at all. If the Church wisely will not contemplate a return to a compartmentalized approach to Sundays, with adults in church and children at Sunday Schools in a hall, with never the two coming together, then it must act to complete the process it has already begun in placing family eucharistic worship at the centre of church life.

Every parent has struggled with the question, often asked at the communion rail itself, 'Why can't I have some, Mummy?' There is no satisfactory answer. If we attempt one in terms of not understanding what it means, we fail to recognize that 'understanding what it means' is a matter of levels of meaning, and who is to say which level is good enough? Have most adults reached that arbitrary level yet? If we attempt an answer in terms of it being somehow too holy, too much of a mystery, we lose sight of the fact that children have an innate reverence that we have lost. The only answer is that the Church says so, and that, as parents know when it is mummy or daddy who say so, is never an answer that will do for long.

The present pattern of worship in the Church of England demands the admission of the baptized to communion. This does not mean permission for experiment in a few places, creating pastoral confusion as people move from church to church, but a national shift that recognizes that sound theology and pastoral needs have come together to make a new practice imperative.

The third affirmation arises from this, but it applies even when children are not communicants. It is that children need not be absent from the Eucharist because of its demands in terms of wonder, awe and mystery. For they have these in greater measure than adults. They do not come with age; if anything they are lost with age. For a child everything has fascination, everything is worth exploring, everything is full of life.

As part of that, children are easily caught up into

mood and atmosphere. If they walk into church and find adults totally gripped and caught up in something full of wonder, something that has taken them over at a deep level, they will not be immune to that atmosphere. They will be quiet. They may even be still if they are entranced. Our problem is not that children have no sense of mystery, but that they do not find it when they come into church. If they are bored and restless, it is often because the adults are not far off boredom and restlessness themselves. It is not so much worship for children that needs to be more full of life and of wonder, but worship for the adults as well.

There are two models of children's participation in the Eucharist. The ideal is not that a church opts for one, but that both models have their place within the pattern of church life. They are both models of 'all age worship', though that term is used more often to describe the first of them.

This is the kind of worship where the whole community remains together throughout the liturgy. Children are present in the church alongside adults from beginning to end, and the style of the service is intended to take the children's needs seriously, but not to disregard the needs of adults also.

The other model is where the community divides for part of the liturgy. Adults and children worship, learn and pray at their own levels, but come together, perhaps at the beginning, certainly at the end, to affirm their unity. For the parts where they are together there is a special sensitivity to the needs of children as well as adults.

Liturgy together

In some churches all age worship, with the whole community staying together throughout the service, is a matter of choice.

Sometimes it arises out of a strong conviction that this ought always to be so. More often it is a conscious decision on one Sunday in each month to bring everyone together, so that those who, on other Sundays, worship and learn at different levels, do not divide on this day, and are joined by a wider community, not present every Sunday, perhaps a parade service of uniformed organizations that also brings in some more adults. This may also be the setting for the celebration of Baptism. Whereas some churches will make the decision that this is a Sunday when the service should not be eucharistic, others will want to keep it so, but in a simple form.

In other churches all age worship of this sort is a necessity, either because there are not the people available to run children's worship and work parallel with the service, or because there is no hall or other room in which parallel activities can take place.

This style of worship, all in together, has much to commend it. Its symbolic value is not to be underestimated. It affirms something fundamental about the nature of the Church. Beyond that, it ensures that families can be together, and sometimes family life needs affirming too. It enables children to know that the Church is their Church now, not something they will one day grow into. It ensures that there will never come a day when they suddenly have to make a move from the security of a Sunday School to the intimidating atmosphere of the 'grown-up church'.

But as a weekly shape to worship, it has its problems. Liturgically it may mean the use week after week of material thought easier for children, to the exclusion of the mainstream liturgical texts of the Church. It may mean a style of preaching so aimed at young people that adults are not receiving the kind of teaching and challenge that will deepen their commitment to Christ. Or the opposite may be so. Because there is a determination that adults shall receive an adult diet, whether in terms of liturgy or of preaching, the children cannot engage with the material.

It may also mean that parents are hardly ever set free from the business of looking after children to be able to concentrate wholeheartedly on worship. For some parents of small children worship is about survival and damage limitation. Yet the parents need nurturing as much as the children.

With all its opportunities and its drawbacks, this is the kind of eucharistic worship to which *Patterns for Worship* is addressed. Its resource material provides good responsive texts, and the freedoms that it envisages (see also Chapter 19) would enable moments that are difficult to handle – the Creed and the Eucharistic Prayer, for instance – to be in a workable form.

Very often, however, the concern is not so much to find resource material, as to make the service shorter. This will sometimes be the wrong concern, for if children are caught up in something, time becomes unimportant. Nevertheless services of this kind do sometimes go on for much longer than is needed. There is a failure to make omissions of unnecessary material. This may be the occasion, for instance, for a liturgy that goes straight from the greeting into prayer and the Collect. It may be the day for a *Patterns for Worship* intercession with minimal local interpolation. It may be the opportunity to streamline the offertory. It may be the time for a swifter method of managing the distribution. It may be the occasion for the briefest form of the concluding section after communion. When people say that the Eucharist is too long for a 'family service', it isn't true. If it is too long, it is because we make it so.

Children are held in the liturgy not only by words and actions to which they can relate, and by a service form that does not make too great a demand on them, but also by being given the opportunity, as much as any adult, to exercise a liturgical ministry. There are few tasks into which children cannot be drawn, often alongside adults. They can sing, play, serve, ring, dance, welcome, collect, and much more, and, if the liturgy is to be their own, they must do these things.

What they are most often asked to do is the thing that many do least well – read the Scriptures and the prayers.

Young people should have a part in this, and sometimes the reading of Scripture will be taken over by them in dramatized form of some sort, but nobody is served by reading that cannot be heard. A token child to read the lesson is a mistake, if the reading is inaudible or the sense lost, and the momentum of the liturgy destroyed. Sometimes the children, as much as the adults, do better to hear the Scriptures through the confident reading of an adult who can tell the story well.

Liturgy at different levels

Most churches will opt if possible for a norm where the community divides for part of the liturgy. This is still an 'all age service', but a recognition that some parts are best celebrated at more than one level.

The moment when all ought to be able to share most easily at the same level is in coming to kneel together at the altar (see above). Any decision about when to divide and when to return together should take that into account. A system that has the children and the adults begin together (with the divide probably at the *Gloria*) but not come back together until the end misses that opportunity.

If the children are to be with the adults at the time of the distribution, when are they to come in? There is a case for their doing so before the Peace, so that the community can be complete before the Ministry of the Sacrament begins. This is better than slipping in under the cover of the offertory hymn. Yet, for young children at least, an adult Eucharistic Prayer, sometimes with fairly elaborate music, does not enthrall. It may be better for them to come in just before the distribution. If they are present for the Lord's Prayer, it is a sensitive touch if the president ensures that it is spoken at a speed in which they can share.

Another factor in deciding when people come and go is that children's activity work requires time. A sense of what was theoretically proper might separate adults

and children only for the Ministry of the Word, in some
churches a matter of twenty-five minutes, but that may
not be long enough for children to settle into their own
activity and derive benefit from it.

There cannot be precise rights and wrongs about
when the community should divide or come together.
But what is important is that it should be seen like that
– a community that worships at different levels, rather
than an adult norm into which children are sometimes
admitted. When they divide, it is not that the children go
for instruction, while the adults stay at worship. The
children's activity is still the liturgy, and still calls for an
atmosphere of celebration, just as much as the adults'.
And when they are divided for a large part of the service,
their liturgy needs to be marked by its songs and its
prayers, as well as its own approach to Scripture and
the learning of the Christian faith. It is 'Sunday
Celebration' more than it is 'Sunday School'.

As to its more precise content, that is beyond the
scope of this book, except to say that, if this really is one
community worshipping at more than one level, there
needs to be overlap in the character of the celebration.
The children's celebration should not sit too lightly to
the Christian year, though it may not need to follow ASB
themes slavishly. When the community comes together,
one half should not be 'coming in cold', so to speak, but
with the material they have been using dovetailing
naturally with what is to follow. It doesn't make sense,
for instance, for children to be building their work
around the Parable of the Sower and then come into the
church to find the adults celebrating the baptism of
Christ. If the children come in, as they may, with a
banner or a model that illustrates what they have been
doing, its reception into the service will cut across the
overall theme of the celebration, and the hymns and
prayers the adults are using will be quite unrelated to
what is in the children's minds.

Sometimes there is a children's 'slot' of some sort
while they are in the church. This has to be handled

with care, for a children's slot can be an excuse for everything else being quite beyond their comprehension. Or it can be the worst sort of patronizing gesture as the children sing (almost inaudibly) a little song that the adults applaud, as if it were a show rather than a liturgy. But, properly handled, this can be a positive moment when the president helps the different parts of the community to relate to one another. He may draw out the connection between what the adults and children have been doing. He may receive from the children something that can contribute genuinely to the total celebration. This may be just before the Peace, though not without some loss to the flow of the service. Often the best point is before the final hymn or song.

A quite different occasion of worshipping at different levels is the Children's Eucharist, a (usually weekday) occasion when children constitute most of the congregation. It may be a School Eucharist or a Children's Club or Youth Club Eucharist. Here quite different conditions apply. Although *Patterns for Worship* begins to address them, on the whole the Church of England, because of its lack of child communicants, has done little thinking and produced few resources. Not so the Roman Church, on whom we have had to rely until now for most of the material at 'Masses for Children'.

Children and the music of the liturgy

Music is the subject of the next chapter, but there is a particular issue concerning music and children in worship. There is today almost no overlap between the music of the average parish church and the average primary school. The problem is not restricted to churches that use only traditional hymnody. There is not much more overlap between the school repertoire and books like *One Hundred Hymns for Today* or *Mission Praise*, except where a Christian member of staff has worked hard to introduce into the school some of the hymns and choruses that the Church uses.

There is no one solution to this problem, certainly not that the Church should cave in, abandon its heritage, and sing only what children know. It may mean a better dialogue between the local church and those responsible for religious education and for music in the local schools. It may mean some time in church devoted to teaching adults and children each other's songs. But it will almost certainly mean a sensitivity about the choice of music at points when children are sharing in worship with adults. If children come in to a difficult tune and complicated words, it is a dreadful start to their experience of that day's liturgy. Yet they are only part of the community, and cannot expect to sing only their songs. Sometimes the younger of them would do better to bring in simple home made musical instruments to accompany the singing than struggle with words beyond their comprehension.

Best of all, everyone, irrespective of age, needs to learn more songs.

22

CELEBRATING WITH MUSIC

Music as ministry

To write in a few words about music at the Eucharist just as the Archbishops' Commission on Church Music publishes its report, *In Tune with Heaven*, may seem a foolishness, and indeed for a proper treatment of this subject the reader needs to turn that report. But there are three principles that come out very clearly in that report, and which have also been fundamental to this book, and they are worth drawing together here.

The first is that the musicians are part of the congregation. Whether traditional choir in its stalls, sometimes through a screen, or newer music group, seated high on its purpose-built dais, there is a constant danger that the musicians will be perceived, or will perceive themselves, as somehow separate and different. Where that feeling is present, it will be difficult for them to make their very special contribution to the building up of the community in its worship. If at all possible, their seating, though it must be determined partly by musical requirements, ought to be such they feel 'part of the congregation'. When the president or other ministers speak, the musicians need to feel that they are being addressed as much as anyone else. Where they are behind the altar or away in a gallery this is not easily achieved.

The second principle is that musicianship, as well as being a gift, is also, in the liturgical context, a ministry. Just as those who arrange flowers, welcome, read or serve, are exercising a ministry in the liturgy, so also are the director of music, the organist, and those who sing or play. It is in many places a demanding ministry, not least in terms of time commitment to services and to practices, and the Church has particular reason to be grateful for the faithfulness with which it is exercised.

The particular ministry that Christian people exercise is not the total of what they bring to worship. The person who reads the lesson is also attentive through the remainder of the service. He or she participates from beginning to end. He or she prays. We would take a poor view (though apparently it happens) if someone came to ring the bells for worship, exercising their distinctive ministry, but then went home, failing to recognize that their membership of the congregation involved not only the ministry of ringing the bells, but also their participation in the entire celebration. Bell-ringers also bring their prayers. So with the musicians. They need to participate in every way, attentive to Scripture and preaching, faithful in prayer and communion, involved in the celebration through spoken parts and through silence, as well as through what is sung.

They need to remember also that every liturgical ministry is a ritual expression of an involvement in the life of the Church through the seven days of the week.

The person who leads the musicians, whether this be director of music, reluctant organist or convenor of an instrumental group, needs to have a particularly clear Christian view of their task as a 'minister of music', for both by teaching and example they have to help their fellow musicians to understand their place in the congregation and the way their gift and ministry contributes to the total celebration.

The third principle, which emerges from the others, is that music is the servant of the liturgy. It is chosen and used for one purpose only, to help the people of God to give God glory, to worship and to pray. When any other motive becomes predominant, wrong choices will be made and the liturgy will not work. Concern that the choir needs stretching with a new setting, or the music group is fed up with a particular song book, or there will be a rebellion if we don't sing this anthem at Harvest because we always do, have to be taken into account, but the primary function of music in worship must not be lost. Its function is, by serving the liturgy, to help the people to draw close to God.

Making choices

For there to be cohesion in the Eucharist, there has to be the right choice of music from beginning to end. The music played before and after the service contributes to the total impact of the celebration as much as the musical 'setting' of the Eucharist itself. The anthem or song the musicians sing alone during the distribution contributes as much as the hymns which the whole congregation sings. And the tune of the hymn is crucial, not just in the sense that it needs to be familiar, but that a hymn takes on a different character when given a different sort of tune. That can be used creatively in the shaping of a service, but the wrong tune can sometimes deny the message of the words or else create a mood the service planners did not intend.

It is very easy to say that the music for all services ought to emerge out of a careful meeting involving the incumbent and the organist or music director, and maybe other clergy involved in the celebration, and perhaps a Worship Group too. That must remain the ideal. But in busy lives, it is not always attainable. There are parishes where the clergy and the musicians do understand one another, and there is a kind of instinct by which one knows what the other wants to achieve. Here less frequent meetings are needed. But at least initially in their relationship clergy and musicians need to devote time to discovering how their understanding of worship and their expertise can be brought together to create good liturgy.

Experience suggests that one of the crucial areas where clergy and musicians need to do more work together is in the developing of the distinctive character of the seasons of the year, the whole area of mood and contrast (discussed in Chapter 7). The impact of more work here on the clergy's choice of hymns and songs and the musician's choice of opening and closing music would in itself be a real source of transformation.

Singing and saying

Every word of worship is to give God glory, but it is also intended to edify the congregation, and it does that by communicating effectively. That needs to be clearly borne in mind as decisions are taken about what is sung and what is said. The fact that in the past the president or deacon sang so much at the Eucharist, even the reading of the Scriptures being sung, was totally in line with this. In vast Gothic buildings, without public address systems, the singing voice carried better than the spoken voice. In some buildings that will still be so. In some buildings less use of a microphone would be a blessing. Communication is the key issue.

At the Eucharist the president and deacon have the option of delegating some musical parts to another (probably lay) minister, whether someone named as 'the cantor' or simply someone in the choir. Singing a responsive penitential *Kyrie* or beginning the *Gloria* are examples where delegation is appropriate. But the president does not delegate the Dialogue or Preface that open the Eucharistic Prayer, nor does the deacon usually delegate the Gospel or the Dismissal (but see Chapter 11). These are integral to their role in the celebration. Where they are not confident or competent singers, they must insist that these parts are spoken, not sung.

The role of the 'cantor' is an interesting one. This is the role of the *animateur* of French liturgy, where it has almost become the ministry of a musical deacon, helping the people through the worship, with a responsive musical style, often unaccompanied, where they repeat what the cantor has sung. There is much possibility for the development of this kind of role, especially in churches where the main (perhaps only) musical resource is a good voice. But, even where the role is not a sustained one throughout the service, the cantor who not only sings the solo parts in a responsorial Psalm or a sung intercession, but develops a style of relating to the congregation to elicit their response more effectively, would be an enrichment to worship.

There is a need for some rethinking about which parts of the eucharistic rite should be sung. Convention, since Holy Communion Series 3, has involved musical settings for *Kyrie, Gloria*, Gospel responses, *Sanctus, Benedictus*, Acclamations in the Eucharistic Prayer, *Agnus Dei* and Dismissal. Churches have wisely made choices about which of these should be sung. Some are too short – responses and Acclamations, for instance – to be very interestingly musically or, where there are several settings in the repertoire, for the people to catch on quickly enough to sing them with the joyful confidence they deserve. There are texts, and these are among them, that are effective when acclaimed confidently with the spoken voice. The leadership of them may still remain with the musical director and choir.

Yet there are other texts, that are assumed to be said, that deserve at least on some occasions to be sung. The case for singing the Creed has already been made (see Chapter 11). The Prayers of Penitence may be sung in the extended *Kyrie* form. So may the Solemn Blessings of the sort in *The Promise of His Glory* and *Enriching the Christian Year*. Above all, there is room for several musical styles in the Prayers of Intercession. There is the well-established tradition of a sung Litany, and that does not need to have the solemn tones of Thomas Tallis. There are also sung texts, more in the Taizé tradition, such as the much-used 'O Lord, hear my prayer' of Jacques Berthier, which can be used either as response to the spoken word, or even as a background to it. The silence that people need at the Eucharist can be enhanced by these gentle repetitive chants to stimulate prayerfulness. The Royal School of Church Music, Kevin Mayhew Ltd and Marshall Pickering, among others, are producing a great deal of new and often simple material that opens up quite new possibilities for music in the Eucharist.

Not only is there benefit in rethinking the balance between what is sung and said at the Eucharist, there is a case also for losing the sharp distinction between a 'Sung Eucharist' and a said one. On a weekday, and without accompaniment, when more than two or three are gathered together, can they not regain the confidence to burst into song, whether it be a hymn at the offertory, a sung doxology to the Eucharistic Prayer, or chant or chorus after communion? They do not need the director of music, the choir or any instrument save their voices to sing the Eucharist.

23

CELEBRATING THROUGH THE WEEK

Experiencing the Eucharist differently

One of the joys of eucharistic worship is the sheer variety of the ways in which it has been experienced (as Gregory Dix expressed in his great 'purple passage' in *The Shape of the Liturgy*). We must be thankful that the form in which most people normally encounter it now is trying to be close to the one that sustained the Church through its early centuries, a participatory celebration of the whole people of God each Sunday, full of vitality and song. But there would be a loss if that 'Parish Communion' style became their only experience of the Eucharist. It is becoming so for many.

Something that is in some danger of being lost is the quiet celebration, which those in the Catholic tradition knew as 'Low Mass', while others talked about 'the 8 o'clock' or 'the early service'. Maybe, as a Sunday option, its days are numbered, even where it has survived till now. But, if that is the case, all the more is the need to provide this different style of eucharistic worship at points through the week. It may be that the Low Mass and the said celebration are an eccentric development of the Eucharist of the primitive Church, but, eccentric or not, they have proved to be channels of grace for many Christians.

In these days, when conflicting loyalties, working hours, family circumstances and other pressures of life make it difficult for everyone to come to church on Sunday morning, the Church should, while holding out the centrality of the 'Lord's service for the Lord's people on the Lord's day', also ensure that there are other opportunities to receive the Ministry of Word and Sacrament.

Both the need to experience the Eucharist differently, and also the need to offer more occasions when it is available, should lead to a stronger provision of weekday eucharistic worship. But the evidence points the other way. It is the exceptional parish where weekday worship is strongly supported, and in parish after parish patterns of weekday worship are collapsing, or are supported only by the elderly.

Daily Communion is not something that most Anglicans have found helpful. But where there is a pattern of daily or frequent eucharistic worship in a parish, it is not there principally for daily communicants, but for a variety of people who will come sometimes, a different congregation every day.

A full pattern of weekday Eucharists is not a viable option in every parish. In one place there isn't the clergy staffing for it, in another the successful pattern of weekday worship and study is not eucharistic, in another the kind of community it is means that very few people would ever be free to come. But there are some other parishes where a return to a richer pattern of weekday worship is only awaiting the commitment and enthusiasm of the parish clergy. Should not most well-staffed clergy teams, and many sizeable town or city parishes, be able to provide this ministry, not only for its own congregation, but for clergy and lay people from surrounding smaller places where it may not be possible to sustain such a pattern?

It would be an enrichment to the Church of England if, alongside the proliferation of house groups, prayer cells and bible studies, which are bringing new life and spiritual vitality in many places, there was also growth in weekday eucharistic worship. It would be a genuine spiritual resource for the whole Church, and not only for those who were present at the celebration. Those who believe this sort of pattern has had its day and has been superseded by the emphasis on Parish Communion are working with too narrow a model of the Eucharist.

One particular Anglican discipline, that seems to be fast disappearing, is the observance of major weekday holy days – 'red letter' days people often called them. Their observance was not restricted by any means to the more Catholic parishes. In the past the majority of clergy would have gathered around them a band of people to celebrate Holy Communion for the Conversion of St Paul, or St Philip and St James, or St Luke, and indeed for a couple of dozen more. Through these days, scattered unevenly through the year, landing sometimes on the most awkward day of the week, churchpeople were enabled to supplement their Sunday spirituality with a different kind of experience of the Eucharist. If this disappears, it will be the loss of another strand of Anglican devotion. There is no need for it to be lost, but it will take clear teaching and patient enthusiasm to restore it in places where it has been neglected.

Daily Eucharist and daily prayer

ASB page 71 provides for the combining of Morning or Evening Prayer with Holy Communion in a service that is both office and Eucharist. There will be times and places where this is right, and without it a community of people sharing both office and Eucharist one after the other can end up with biblical indigestion. This book has tried to make clear and attractive the particular shape and character of the Eucharist. At much the same time the quite different shape and character of Morning and Evening Prayer is being made clear and attractive in the publication of *Celebrating Common Prayer* (Mowbray 1992). If both these books are right, the Church has two forms of daily worship, with overlap certainly, but quite distinctive, each sufficiently rich better to stand alone. Ideally office and Eucharist should not follow one another, but be at different times.

In some communities, and some individual clergy lives, that is more possible than in others. Where office and Eucharist have to be together, it will often be better to bring material from one and integrate it into the clear shape and structure of the other, rather than, as in ASB, attempting to combine two structures. Thus, if ASB office material is to be drawn into the Eucharist,

> its invitatory Psalm or one of its canticles begins the rite,
>
> its readings become the readings for the Eucharist,
>
> its Psalms are read between the readings,
>
> its Morning or Evening Collect becomes a prayer after communion.

Where its second reading is not from one of the Gospels, Morning and Evening Prayer lections will need to be reversed so that there is a gospel reading.

Weekday style

The style of the weekday Eucharist will depend very much on whether it is a service shared each day by the same people or one where the congregation is different each day of the week.

Where it is the same people who gather each day, they will benefit from the reading of Scripture in some sort of sequence, probably following the ASB's Daily Eucharistic Lectionary, based on the Roman one. When this happens there is a good case for using the sequence of collects in *Celebrating Common Prayer*, rather than the ASB's set that is tied to the Sunday themes. When it is the same congregation each day, it will also make sense to use material like the *Gloria* and Creed minimally. Intercession will not need to draw in *everything* every day as if it were the only intercession of the week.

But, when there are different people every day, the need may be a different one. Sequential reading of

Scripture makes less sense, and a wider use of all the options in the Sunday provision may be a better way forward. If, for some, those who work on Sunday for instance, or the elderly unable to be up in time for the main Sunday celebration, this is the only service of the week, the president may need to be more generous in including optional material that they would otherwise entirely miss. The pastoral will dictate the form, as much as the liturgical. It may also influence which rite is used.

However, there is no need for weekday celebrations to be unimaginative. If questions such as posture, lay participation, psalmody, homily and the use of silence have been rethought in relation to the Sunday liturgy, what has been learnt need not be ignored in relation to weekdays. In addition, the smaller celebration has possibilities that are not present in bigger services. At the Peace, for instance, the people might come out of their places and gather around the altar in a circle or semi-circle for the Eucharistic Prayer and the communion, only returning to their places for the silent prayer that follows the distribution.

What is also important at these quieter weekday celebrations, at which numbers will not often be large, is that those who come to bring not only their own needs and satisfy their own souls, but also have a sense of praying for the community, and holding up to God the everyday world.

24

CELEBRATING FOR THE WORLD

Sanctifying the creation

When thinking about the Eucharist section by section, and trying to get the detail right so that the liturgy may make people more open to the Spirit, it is easy to lose sight of the broader picture. It is to that picture that I want to return in these last pages, and to make two affirmations about the Eucharist in the world.

The first is that the celebration of the Eucharist is always a bringing to God of needs far beyond those of the congregation, however large or small, that is gathered together. It is always for the community, and it is, in a sense, always for the whole creation.

Every offering of penitence, prayer and praise is that. It is not only through the Eucharist that the world is drawn to God. The individual praying of every Christian ought to have that dimension that looks beyond self, and the celebration of the Church's daily office, its corporate prayer, morning and evening, has the same quality, and through the intercession, which is its classic climax, brings to God prayer that is always on behalf of a much wider constituency than those who share its recitation.

But never is that prayerful offering up of the creation to its Maker and Sustainer more tellingly expressed than in the Eucharist. In the Eucharist we come, with our spiritual hunger, and are fed with the Bread of Life. We ritualize and celebrate God's response to human need. We bring him his world, which hungers for his life-giving word, and in our communion we taste and see how he feeds and satisfies.

In the Eucharist we call down the Spirit which touches

and transforms, not only bread and wine, but people and relationships. The Spirit makes people holy and equips them with gifts of many kinds. The Spirit also flows between them, healing and renewing their relationships one with another. We pray,

> pour out your Holy Spirit over us and these your gifts, which we bring before you from your own creation.

We focus the renewing power of the Spirit in the Eucharist, but know that to be a sign that the Spirit, who hovered over the waters at the creation, fills the whole universe, and is at work in every human soul and in the relationships between them, especially where love, peace and healing are flowing from one to another.

In the Eucharist we celebrate how God is at work in the world of matter. Our eyes are on bread and wine, fruits of the creation, and even they sing his praises. As the first Eucharistic Prayer in *Patterns for Worship* expresses it:

> The created universe itself praises you, its Creator.
> Sun and rain, hills and rivers praise you.
> The fruit of the earth itself praises you:
> Wheat and grape, this bread and wine,
> are part of the riches of your earth.

Yet it does not stop there. The primary significance of the creation in the Eucharist, of which the bread and wine are symbols, is not in what it does, but in what God does. It is not the creation's praising, but God's sanctifying, that is at the heart of the rite. God, who is holy indeed, the source of all holiness, by the power of his Spirit makes them holy. It is in that sense that as they celebrate the Eucharist, with bread and wine upon the table, Christians can hold on to a cosmic view of the whole creation, with all its goodness and its pain, being renewed by the Spirit of God.

Yet none of these three overlapping eucharistic images – of hunger being satisfied, of the Spirit at work in people and between them, of the creation being made holy – come quite to the heart of the matter. There is something more, and indeed without this final truth the others could easily degenerate into sentiment and false doctrine.

At the heart is the cross. The Eucharist is the form of prayer in which we bring the world to God most tellingly because it is the Eucharist that sets forth the sacrifice that takes away the sins of the world and reconciles the human race to God. For the touch of God in making the bread and wine holy is, more precisely, in making them for us the Body of Christ, that was given, and the Blood of Christ, which was shed for all that sins might be forgiven. So, in coming with the world on their hearts to the altar, Christian people are recognizing the world's need for redemption, and bringing it, as far as they are able, to the cross where that redemption is found.

In that sense we celebrate the Eucharist for the world.

A rite that converts

I believe also that the Eucharist is for the world in the sense that God has made it a marvellous tool in the work of evangelism, in drawing people into faith. That view has been going out of fashion. The Eucharist is seen as too 'churchy' to speak to those on its fringe and those still to commit themselves, and services are devised that make less demand of people, are more easily intelligible, and meet them where they are. That is an absolutely right thing to do, and the Church needs to develop that art imaginatively. But, alongside it, it must not lose its faith in the Eucharist, in John Wesley's phrase, as 'a converting ordinance'.

This book began with the belief that our only motive for worship has to be worship itself, the desire and need to give God glory. I believe that worship is about the overwhelming reality of God and of his holiness, about glimpses of heaven that are ours for the prayerful asking, and that we are selling people short if we expect less.

But I do believe in the power of the liturgy to make new Christians.

It happens because people, whose hearts God has been preparing, come into our worship, which very likely they don't understand (certainly not all the rich levels of meaning that we know are there), but they hear the story of the world's salvation powerfully retold and celebrated in word and sacrament, they encounter Jesus Christ among his people as the Church worships in truth and fellowship, and they too catch a glimpse of heaven, as the Church strains to join its praises with the angels and the archangels.

That does not alter the fact that what the Church has to work at is offering worship; worship, moreover, that is true, sincere, from the heart, full of faith, genuine communication with the living God revealed in Jesus Christ. The Church does not set out to evangelize through worship. It sets out to worship, but if its worship is authentic, then it will convert. Be it through the simple Communion of a house group, or through the Schubert Mass and the clouds of smoke of a Solemn Eucharist in a great cathedral, or through the ordinary weekly or daily celebration in any parish church across the land, if the reality of the relationship between God and the worshippers is almost tangible, if it is indeed a lively sacrifice, it will convert.

BIBLIOGRAPHY

Books referred to in the text:

Lent, Holy Week, Easter: Services and Prayers. Church House Publishing/Cambridge University Press/SPCK 1986.

The Promise of His Glory: Services and Prayers for the Season from All Saints to Candlemas. Mowbray/Church House Publishing 1991.

Patterns for Worship. Church House Publishing 1989.

Making Women Visible: The Use of Inclusive Language with the ASB. Church House Publishing 1988.

Concelebration in the Eucharist GS Misc 163. Church House Publishing 1982.

In Tune with Heaven: The Report of the Archbishops' Commission on Church Music. Church House Publishing/Hodder & Stoughton 1992.

Celebrating Common Prayer. Mowbray 1992.

The Book of Alternative Services of the Anglican Church in Canada. Anglican Book Centre Toronto 1985.

Charles MacDonnell *After Communion*. Mowbray 1985.

Michael Perham *Liturgy Pastoral and Parochial*. SPCK 1984.

Michael Perham, ed. *Enriching the Christian Year*. SPCK 1993.

Michael Perry, ed. *The Dramatised Bible*. Marshall Pickering/Bible Society 1989.

ACKNOWLEDGEMENTS

The author and publishers are pleased to acknowledge the following for permission to quote from their copyright material:

The Central Board of Finance of the Church of England for extracts from *Lent, Holy Week, Easter: Services and Prayers* © 1984, 1986; *Patterns for Worship*: A Report by the Liturgical Commission © 1989; *The Alternative Service Book* © 1980 and from *The Promise of His Glory* © 1990, 1991.

Extracts from *The Book of Common Prayer*, the rights in which are vested in the Crown, are reproduced by permission of the Crown's Patentee, Cambridge University Press.

INDEX

There are no entries in this Index for Jesus Christ, worship, Church of England, *The Book of Common Prayer*, *The Alternative Service Book 1980*, Holy Communion Rite A, altar, president, priest, hymn and song because references to them occur throughout the text.